Letters from the Battlefront

The Revolutionary War

VIRGINIA SCHOMP

BENCHMARK BOOKS

MARSHALL CAVENDISH
NEW YORK

To Nancy Schomp, an American Original

Benchmark Books
Marshall Cavendish
99 White Plains Road
Tarrytown, New York 10591-9001
www.marshallcavendish.com

Library of Congress Cataloging-in-Publication Data

Schomp, Virginia.
The Revolutionary War / by Virginia Schomp.
p. cm. — (Letters from the battlefront)
Summary: Describes the Revolutionary War through the letters of the people who fought it, including both British and Americans, Loyalists and Patriots, women, and Native Americans.
Includes bibliographical references and index.
ISBN 0-7614-1659-5
1. United States—History—Revolution, 1775-1783—Personal narratives—Juvenile literature. [1. United States—History—Revolution, 1775-1783—Personal narratives.] I. Title. II. Series.

E275.A2S36 2003
973.3'092'2—dc21   2003001476

Book design by Patrice Sheridan
Art Research: Rose Corbett Gordon & Alexandra H.C. Gordon, Mystic CT
Cover: Christie's Images/Corbis
Art Resource, NY: page 66; The Connecticut Historical Society, Hartford: p.28; The Granger Collection, New York: pages 9, 15, 16, 18, 21, 43, 44, 47, 48, 53, 54, 55, 59, 64, 65, 70, 71, 72, 74 & 78; Hulton Archive/Getty Images: page 23; Scala/Art Resource, NY: pages 12, 30, & 37; Smithsonian American Art Museum/Art Resource, NY: pages 34 & 80.

Printed in China
1 3 5 6 4 2

A Note on Editing

In order to preserve the "personality" and historic accuracy of the letters and other writings in this book, we have done as little editing as possible. Many people in Revolutionary War times did not follow any standard rules for spelling, capitalization, or punctuation, but in most cases we have not modernized the resulting oddities of style. We have occasionally added words in brackets to make meanings clear. Ellipses (. . .) show where words have been dropped.

Contents

From the Author

Letters from the Battlefront is written as a companion to the *Letters from the Homefront* series. The books in that series told the story of America's wars from the viewpoint of those who worked, watched, and waited at home. These books look at the same conflicts through the eyes of the men and women on the front lines.

Historians often study letters and journals written by famous people—explorers, philosophers, kings—to gain information about the past. Recently they have discovered the value of writings by "ordinary" people, too. Students of history have begun to seek out and study the personal writings of farmers and merchants, slaves and slaveholders, sailors and foot soldiers. Documents such as these, often called primary sources, help us to understand the beliefs, hopes, and dreams of earlier generations and to learn how historical events shaped their lives.

This book uses primary sources to recapture the drama of life during the American Revolution. In these pages you will hear the words of both Patriots and Loyalists. You will meet the militiamen who volunteered to fight for liberty, the Continental soldiers who shivered and starved at Valley Forge, the privateersmen who sailed the high seas, and the leaders who struggled to shape and preserve an infant nation. Their letters, journals, and reflections on war bring alive the extraordinary years that saw the birth of a new republic based on principles of liberty and equality that continue to inspire the world.

Introduction

The Seeds of Revolution

In 1763 American colonists thought of themselves as proud and loyal British subjects. Thirteen years later, they would be fighting a bitter, bloody war for independence. What were the conflicts that turned loyalty into armed rebellion?

The seeds of revolution were planted in the French and Indian War. From 1754 to 1763 the British fought the French and their Native American allies for control of territories in North America. Britain won the war. It gained control of a vast area from the Atlantic Ocean to the Mississippi River, and all of Canada. But the war left Britain deeply in debt, and the British decided that the colonists should pay their fair share.

"No taxation without representation!" That was the American response when Britain tried to raise money through new taxes. The colonists were used to collecting and spending taxes through their own assemblies. They had no representatives in the British Parliament, so they believed that Parliament had no right to tax them. They were especially outraged in 1765, when Britain passed the Stamp Act. That act taxed the colonists by making them buy a government stamp for all printed materials—newspapers, wills, diplomas, marriage certificates, even playing cards. At town meetings throughout the thirteen colonies, Americans agreed to boycott British goods in protest. Groups calling themselves the Sons of Liberty were organized to "persuade" stamp agents to

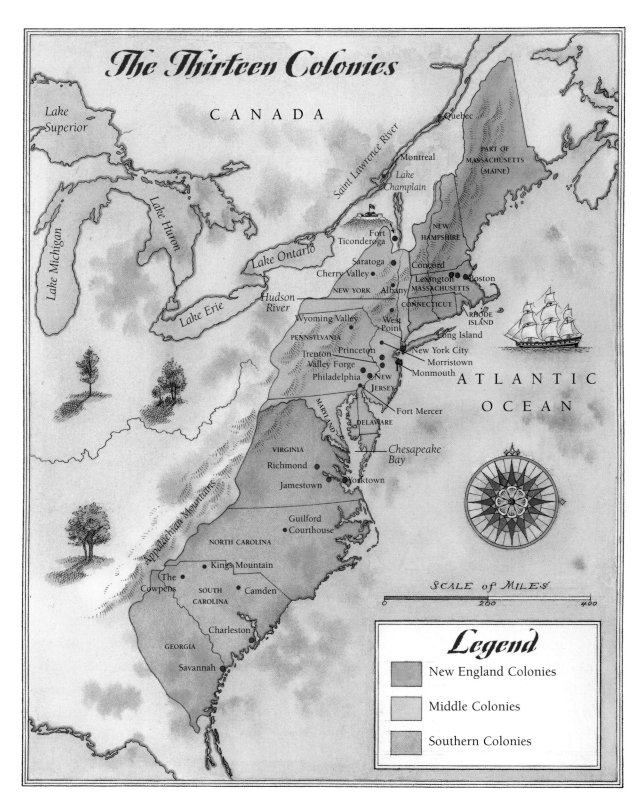

The Thirteen Colonies

CANADA

Lake Superior

Lake Michigan

Lake Huron

Lake Ontario

Lake Erie

Saint Lawrence River

Quebec

Montreal

Lake Champlain

PART OF MASSACHUSETTS (MAINE)

Fort Ticonderoga

Saratoga

Cherry Valley

NEW HAMPSHIRE

Concord

Lexington

Boston

Albany

MASSACHUSETTS

Hudson River

NEW YORK

CONNECTICUT

RHODE ISLAND

Wyoming Valley

West Point

Long Island

PENNSYLVANIA

Trenton

Princeton

New York City

Valley Forge

Morristown

Philadelphia

Monmouth

NEW JERSEY

Fort Mercer

MARYLAND

DELAWARE

ATLANTIC OCEAN

Chesapeake Bay

VIRGINIA

Richmond

Jamestown

Yorktown

Appalachian Mountains

Guilford Courthouse

NORTH CAROLINA

Kings Mountain

The Cowpens

SOUTH CAROLINA

Camden

Charleston

GEORGIA

Savannah

SCALE of MILES

0   200   400

Legend

New England Colonies

Middle Colonies

Southern Colonies

resign—sometimes with threats, sometimes with violence. Finally Britain was forced to repeal the Stamp Act.

More taxes—and more protests—followed. In 1768 the British tried to restore order by sending seven hundred red-uniformed soldiers to Boston, a center of the resistance movement. The Bostonians hated the Redcoats. Tensions mounted, leading to bloodshed. On March 5, 1770, a group of British soldiers fired into a mob that was pelting them with rocks and icy snowballs. Five Americans were killed. The Sons of Liberty quickly spread the news of the "Boston Massacre."

The next big confrontation came in 1773. To protest a British tax on tea, a group of colonists thinly disguised as Indians boarded three tea ships in Boston Harbor and dumped their cargoes into the water. In response to the Boston Tea Party, Parliament passed its toughest measures to date. A series of new laws that colonists labeled the Intolerable Acts closed Boston Harbor and sharply restricted the powers of the Massachusetts colonial government. Redcoats flooded into Boston, turning the city into an armed camp.

All these actions outraged the colonists. In September 1774 the First Continental Congress met in Philadelphia to decide on a response. The delegates declared the rights of Americans to pass their own laws and taxes. They urged citizens to arm themselves for a possible military showdown. Colonists had already begun training on village greens and hiding stockpiles of weapons and ammunition. "War is inevitable," cried Patriot leader Patrick Henry of Virginia. "Let it come! . . . I know not what course others may take, but as for me, give me liberty or give me death!"

One

The Shot Heard
'Round the World

When I reflect and consider that the fight was between those
whose parents but a few generations ago were brothers,
I shudder at the thought.

—JOHN ADAMS, APRIL 19, 1775

Lexington and Concord

As the spirit of rebellion spread through the colonies, Britain made plans to squash it. General Thomas Gage, commander of British forces in America, learned that the rebels were stockpiling weapons in Concord, eighteen miles from Boston. Gage decided to send seven hundred troops on a secret nighttime march to seize and destroy the supplies.

His plan wasn't secret for long. The rebels had an efficient network of spies watching every move the British made. As the Redcoats prepared to leave Boston, two riders, Paul Revere and William Dawes, galloped across the countryside, raising the

Militiamen and Redcoats fire the first shots of the Revolutionary War, in Lexington, Massachusetts, April 19, 1775.

alarm. At dawn on April 19, 1775, when the weary British soldiers reached Lexington, on the road to Concord, about seventy colonial militiamen were waiting. A shot rang out, then a whole volley of musket fire. Eight Americans lay dead or dying.

NO ONE KNOWS WHO FIRED THE FIRST SHOT OF THE REVOLUTIONARY WAR. EACH SIDE BLAMED THE OTHER. HERE IS ONE ACCOUNT OF THE BATTLE OF LEXINGTON, PRESENTED IN A REPORT TO GENERAL GAGE BY LIEUTENANT-COLONEL FRANCIS SMITH, THE LEADER OF THE BRITISH EXPEDITION.

Boston, April 22, 1775

SIR,—In obedience to your Excellency's commands, I marched on the evening of the 18th . . . with the corps of grenadiers and light infantry for Concord, to execute your Excellency's orders with respect to destroying all ammunition, artillery, tents, &c. [etc.], collected there. . . . Notwithstanding we marched with the utmost expedition [speed] and secrecy, we found the country had intelligence or strong suspicion of our coming, and fired many signal guns, and rung the alarm bells repeatedly; and were informed, when at Concord, that some cannon had been taken out of the town that day, that others, with some stores [supplies], had been carried three days before, which prevented our having an opportunity of destroying so much as might have been expected at our first setting off.

I think it proper to observe, that when I had got some miles on the march from Boston, I detached six light infantry companies to march with all expedition to seize the two bridges on different roads beyond Concord. On these companies' arrival at Lexington, . . . they found on a green close to the road a body of the country people drawn up in military order, with arms and accoutrements [equipment], and, as appeared after, loaded; and that they had posted some men in a dwelling and Meeting-house. Our troops advanced towards them, without any intention of injuring them, further than to inquire the reason of their being thus assembled, and, if not satisfactory, to have secured their arms; but they in confusion went off, principally to the left, only one of them fired before he went off, and three or four more jumped over a wall and fired from behind it among the soldiers; on which the troops returned it, and killed several of them. . . .

I have the honour, &c.,
F. Smith, Lieutenant-Colonel 10th Foot

April 19, 1776

Between the hours of twelve and one, on the morning of the nineteenth of April, we received intelligence . . . "that a large body of the king's troops (supposed to be a brigade of about 12 or 1500) were embarked . . . from Boston." . . .

The militia of this town were alarmed and ordered to meet on the usual place. . .

About half an hour after four o'clock, alarm guns were fired, and the drums beat to arms, and the militia were collecting together. . . . In the mean time, the troops . . . seemed to come determined for murder and bloodshed—and that whether provoked to it or not! When within about half a quarter of a mile of the meeting-house, they halted, and the command was given to prime and load; which being done, they marched on till they came up to the east end of said meeting-house, in sight of our militia. . . .

Immediately upon their appearing so suddenly and so nigh [near], Capt. [John] Parker, who commanded the militia company, ordered the men to disperse and take care of themselves, and not to fire. Upon this, our men dispersed—but many of them not so speedily as they might have done, not having the most distant idea of such brutal barbarity and more than savage cruelty from the troops of a British king. . .

About the same time, three officers . . . advanced on horse back to the front of the body, and coming within 5 or 6 rods of the militia, one of them cried out, "Ye villains, ye Rebels, disperse! Damn you, disperse!"—or words to this effect. . . . The second of these officers, about this time, fired a pistol towards the militia as they were dispersing. The foremost, . . . brandishing his sword and then pointing toward them, with a loud voice said to the troops, "Fire! By God, fire!"—which was instantly followed by a discharge of arms from the said troops, succeeded by a very heavy and close fire upon our party, dispersing, so long as any of them were within reach. Eight were left dead upon the ground! Ten were wounded. The rest of the company, through divine goodness, were (to a miracle) preserved unhurt in this murderous action!

Two Kinds of Soldiers

The Americans who answered the first call to arms of the Revolutionary War were militiamen. Each of the thirteen colonies had a militia. These citizen armies included all able-bodied men between the ages of sixteen and sixty. Militiamen were required to own a gun and to meet a few times a year to practice some basic battle formations. A few handpicked units of militiamen were specially trained as minutemen. The minutemen drilled several hours a week and were expected to be "ready to act at a minute's warning."

The militiamen fought bravely at Lexington and Concord, but they were inexperienced and unreliable soldiers who came and went as they pleased. The Continental Congress knew that the colonies needed a regular army to face Britain's well-trained forces. It called for each colony to organize regiments to fight in the new Continental army. Continental soldiers differed from the militiamen in two important ways: they had to stay for their full term of enlistment, and they had to serve anywhere fighting occurred, not just in their own home regions.

In time, the militias and the Continental army worked together to make a strong and effective fighting force. As one historian sums it up, "The militia could not have won the war alone—but the war probably could not have been won without them."

A Revolutionary minuteman holds his musket. The minutemen were the best-trained soldiers in the colonies' citizen armies.

The British continued on to Concord, where they found few supplies—most had already been moved out of town or hidden. There was a brief exchange of gunfire. Then, around noon, the Redcoats began the long march back to Boston.

By now the whole countryside was up in arms. Roused by church bells and signal guns, more than four thousand militiamen lay in wait alongside the road. "We were fired at from all quarters," one British lieutenant wrote in his diary,

> but particularly from the houses on the roadside, and the adjacent stone walls. . . . During the whole of the march from Lexington the Rebels kept an incessant [nonstop] irregular fire from all points at the column. . . . They hardly ever fired but under cover of a stone wall, from behind a tree, or out of a house; and the moment they had fired they lay down out of sight.

By the time the Redcoats stumbled into Boston that night, about 90 colonists and 275 British soldiers had been killed or wounded. The Revolutionary War had begun.

The Second Continental Congress

Three weeks after the Battles of Lexington and Concord, the Second Continental Congress met in Philadelphia. The delegates had good news to discuss. Militiamen led by Benedict Arnold and Ethan Allen had captured Fort Ticonderoga, a British stronghold in northern New York. Nearly one hundred artillery pieces had been captured—a valuable haul for the poorly armed rebel army.

There were also difficult decisions to make. Blood had been shed but no war declared. Moderate delegates hoped to avoid an all-out revolution, while radicals were ready to fight. The divided Congress ended up issuing two contradictory documents. The Olive Branch Petition asked Britain's King George III for a peaceful settlement of differences. The Declaration of the Causes and Necessity of Taking Up Arms justified military resistance against Britain's "cruel aggression."

Both moderates and radicals agreed on one point: the colonies must be prepared to defend themselves. America needed a trained army of men from all the colonies. To lead that Continental army, the delegates chose a respected Patriot, George Washington.

HISTORIANS AGREE THAT AMERICA PROBABLY WOULD NOT HAVE WON ITS REVOLUTION WITHOUT GEORGE WASHINGTON. A TALL, QUIET GENTLEMAN FARMER FROM VIRGINIA, WASHINGTON HAD SERVED WITH THE MILITIA DURING THE FRENCH AND INDIAN WAR. MUCH OF HIS SUCCESS AS A MILITARY COMMANDER CAME FROM HIS ABILITY TO INSPIRE LOYALTY THROUGH HIS QUIET CONFIDENCE, DEVOTION TO DUTY, AND DEEP COMMITMENT TO THE WELFARE OF HIS MEN. WASHINGTON ACCEPTED HIS APPOINTMENT AS COMMANDER-IN-CHIEF OF THE CONTINENTAL ARMY RELUCTANTLY. IN THIS LETTER TO HIS WIFE, MARTHA (NICKNAMED PATCY), HE EXPRESSES HIS CONCERN THAT HE WILL NOT BE EQUAL TO THE DIFFICULT TASK AHEAD.

Philadelphia June 18th, 1775

My Dearest,

I am now set down to write to you on a subject which fills me with inexpressible concern— and this concern is greatly aggravated and Increased when I reflect on the uneasiness I know it will give you—It has been determined in Congress, that the whole Army raised for the defence of the American Cause shall be put under my care, and that it is necessary for me to proceed immediately to Boston to take upon me the Command of it. You may believe me my dear Patcy, when I assure you, in the most solemn manner, that, so far from seeking this appointment I have used every endeavor in my power to avoid it, not only from my unwillingness to part with you and the Family, but from a consciousness of its being a trust too great for my Capacity and that I should enjoy more real happiness and felicity in one month with you, at home, than I have the most distant prospect of reaping abroad, if my stay was to be Seven times Seven years. But, as it has been a kind of destiny that has thrown me upon this Service, I shall hope that my undertaking of it, is designd to answer some good purpose. . . . It was utterly out of my power to refuse this appointment without exposing my Character to such censures [criticism] as would have reflected dishonour upon myself, and given pain to my friends—this I am sure could not, and ought not to be pleasing to you, & must have lessend me considerably in my own esteem. I shall rely therefore, confidently, on that Providence which has heretofore preservd, & been bountiful to me, not doubting but that I shall return safe to you in the fall. . . .

I am with most unfeigned regard, My dear Patcy Yr Affecte
Go: Washington

George Washington accepts his appointment as general and commander-in-chief of the Continental army, at the Second Continental Congress, June 15, 1775.

Battle of Bunker Hill

Before Washington even had time to start building his army, the bloodiest battle of the American Revolution was fought. Militiamen had been pouring into the Boston area ever since Lexington and Concord. By June 1775 some 14,000 Americans had the city under siege. The British decided it was time to strike back against the rebels' "preposterous parade of military arrangement."

The colonists made their stand on Breed's Hill, a high point on the Charlestown Peninsula, across from Boston. (Although the fighting took place on Breed's Hill, this clash is traditionally called the Battle of Bunker Hill, after a neighboring height.) Twice a massive force of Redcoats charged up the hill; twice they were

British troops marched in ranks toward rebel positions in the Battle of Bunker Hill. "They looked too handsome to be fired at," recalled one young militiaman, "but we had to do it."

mowed down by musket fire. On the third attempt the rebels ran out of ammunition. Thomas Jones, a Boston judge loyal to the British, reported that

> the rebels hove down their guns, took to their heels and made their escape, leaving about 300 killed and wounded. . . . Alas, a dear bought victory it was. Not less than 1,200 as brave Britons as ever entered the field were, on that unfortunate day either killed or wounded.

The British had won the Battle of Bunker Hill. But in the process, an outnumbered, ragtag army of militiamen had proven they could hold their own against King George's finest forces. "If we have eight more such victories," commented one man in London, "there will be nobody left to bring the news of them."

"Time to Part"

Through the winter of 1775-1776, the tidings of war filtered into the Continental Congress, still meeting in Philadelphia. First came the news that King George had refused to even read the Olive Branch Petition, instead issuing a proclamation that declared the colonies in open rebellion. Next came word of the disastrous defeat of American forces led by Benedict Arnold and Richard Montgomery against the British at Quebec.

BENEDICT ARNOLD IS AMERICA'S MOST FAMOUS TRAITOR, BUT IN THE EARLY YEARS OF THE REVOLUTION, HE WAS KNOWN AS A BRAVE AND DARING HERO. IN THE WINTER OF 1775, ARNOLD LED A GROUP OF 1,100 VOLUNTEERS FROM MASSACHUSETTS TO QUEBEC, CANADA. THE MEN SUFFERED INCREDIBLE HARDSHIPS ON THEIR FORTY-FIVE-DAY TREK THROUGH SNOW, HIP-DEEP SWAMPS, AND MILES OF ICY RIVER. IN THIS LETTER TO AMERICAN GENERAL PHILIP SCHUYLER, ARNOLD DESCRIBES THE NIGHTMARISH MARCH. ALTHOUGH HE EXPRESSES CONFIDENCE IN THE PLANNED ATTACK ON THE BRITISH FORT AT QUEBEC, THE VENTURE WOULD END IN FAILURE, WITH SIXTY AMERICANS KILLED AND MORE THAN FOUR HUNDRED CAPTURED.

Pointe Aux Trembles, November 27, 1775

. . . Thus in about eight weeks we completed a march of near six hundred miles, not to be paralleled in history; the men having with the greatest fortitude and perseverance hauled their batteaux [boats] up rapid streams, being obliged to wade almost the whole way, near 180 miles, carried them on their shoulders near forty miles, over hills, swamps and bogs almost impenetrable, and to their knees in mire; being often obliged to cross three or four times with their baggage. Short of provisions, part of the detachment disheartened and gone back; famine staring us in the face; an enemy's country and uncertainty ahead. Notwithstanding all these obstacles, the officers and men, inspired and fired with the love of liberty and their country, pushed on with a fortitude superior to every obstacle, and most of them had not one day's provision for a week.

Thus I have given you a short but imperfect sketch of our march. The night we crossed the St. Lawrence [River], found it impossible to get our ladders over, and the enemy being apprised of our coming, we found it impracticable to attack them without too great a risk; we therefore invested [surrounded] the town and cut off their communication with the country. . . . On a strict scrutiny into our ammunition, found many of our cartridges (which to appearance were good) inserviceable and not ten rounds each for the men, who were almost naked, bare footed and much fatigued; and as the garrison was daily increasing and nearly double our number, we thought it prudent to retire to this place and wait the arrival of Gen. Montgomery, with artillery, clothing, etc., who to our great joy has this morning joined us with about 300 men. We propose immediately investing the town and make no doubt in a few days to bring [the British] to terms. . . .

Benedict Arnold

Much better news came in March. Under George Washington's command, the artillery captured at Fort Ticonderoga had been secretly transported to Boston and positioned on Dorchester Heights, overlooking the city. One morning the Redcoats awoke to find fifty-nine cannons bearing down on them. "Good God," exclaimed the new British commander General William Howe, "these fellows have done more work in one night than I could have made my army do in three months." Howe feared that an assault on the heights would end in another slaughter like Bunker Hill. On March 17, 1776, the British troops boarded ships and evacuated Boston.

Congress awarded Washington a gold medal. Then the delegates went back to arguing.

Their divisions were sharper than ever. Radicals such as Samuel Adams and Patrick Henry had begun to speak of independence, but most delegates still recoiled from the idea. They continued to hope for "a restoration of the state of things before

Thomas Paine, author of the famous 1776 pamphlet Common Sense

the contest began." Britain's actions were wrong and must be resisted, they argued, but breaking away would be suicide. As one statesman put it, "Our own happiness, our very being, depend upon our being connected with our Mother Country."

It was about this time that a new voice entered the debate. Thomas Paine was an Englishman who had come to Philadelphia and thrown himself into the Patriot cause. In his pamphlet *Common Sense,* Paine used bold, persuasive language to present the case for independence.

> Britain is the parent country, say some. Then the more shame upon her conduct. Even brutes do not devour their young, nor savages make war upon their families. . . . The blood of the slain, the weeping voice of nature cries, 'TIS TIME TO PART. . . .
>
> O! ye that love mankind! Ye that dare oppose not only the tyranny but the tyrant, stand forth! Freedom hath been hunted round the globe. . . . O! receive the fugitive, and prepare in time an asylum for mankind.

Common Sense sold 120,000 copies in three months—a huge number for those times. The soldiers camped outside Boston passed dog-eared copies from hand to hand, and in the South, one man noted, people spoke of nothing "but *Common Sense* and independency." Another colonist wrote to John Adams to ask why Congress was so slow to follow "the dictates of common sense."

The Declaration of Independence

In the spring of 1776, mud-splattered riders galloped into Philadelphia, carrying resolutions from the colonial assemblies. One by one nearly all the colonies instructed their delegates to vote for independence. Thomas Jefferson, a young Virginia lawyer known for his "happy talent of composition," was given the job of preparing a statement to bring together all the separate resolutions.

Jefferson labored for two weeks, writing and rewriting. In June his Declaration was presented to Congress. The delegates debated, added lines, took out paragraphs. Finally, on July 4, Congress approved the final version of the Declaration of Independence.

JOHN ADAMS WAS ONE OF THE FIRST PATRIOT LEADERS TO CALL FOR INDEPENDENCE. HERE HE SENDS HIS WIFE, ABIGAIL, THE EXCITING NEWS OF CONGRESS'S VOTE FOR INDEPENDENCE ON JULY 2, 1776. ADAMS'S PREDICTION THAT THE DATE OF THAT VOTE WOULD BE CELEBRATED AS AMERICA'S BIRTHDAY TURNED OUT TO BE WRONG—CONGRESS WOULD SPEND TWO MORE DAYS TINKERING WITH THE DECLARATION OF INDEPENDENCE BEFORE FORMALLY ADOPTING IT ON THE FOURTH OF JULY.

Philadelphia, July 3, 1776

. . . Yesterday the greatest Question was decided, which ever was debated in America, and a greater perhaps, never was or will be decided among Men. A Resolution was passed without one dissenting Colony "that these united Colonies, are, and of right ought to be free and independent States. . . ." You will see in a few days a Declaration setting forth the Causes, which have impell'd Us to this mighty Revolution, and the Reasons which will justify it, in the Sight of God and Man. A Plan of Confederation will be taken up in a few days.

When I look back to the year 1761, . . . and run through the whole Period from that Time to this, and recollect the series of political Events, the Chain of Causes and Effects, I am surprized at the Suddenness, as well as the Greatness of this Revolution. Britain has been fill'd with Folly, and America with Wisdom, at least this is my Judgment.—Time must determine. It is the will of Heaven, that the two Countries should be sundered forever. It may be the Will of Heaven that America shall suffer Calamities still more wasting and Distresses yet more dreadfull—if this is to be the Case, it will have this good Effect, at least: it will inspire Us with many Virtues, which We have not, and correct many Errors, Follies, and Vices, which threaten to disturb, dishonour, and destroy Us. . . .

The second day of July 1776, will be the most memorable Epocha [date] in the history of America.—I am apt to believe that it will be celebrated, by succeeding Generations, as the great anniversary Festival. It ought to be commemorated, as the Day of Deliverance by solemn Acts of Devotion to God Almighty. It ought to be solemnized with Pomp and Parade, with Shews [shows], Games, Sports, Guns, Bells, Bonfires and Illuminations from one End of this Continent to the other from this Time forward forever more.

You will think me transported with Enthusiasm but I am not.—I am well aware of the Toil and Blood and Treasure, that it will cost Us to maintain this Declaration, and support and defend these States.—Yet through all the Gloom I can see the Rays of ravishing Light and Glory.

George Washington (on the white horse) *gathers his troops for a reading of the Declaration of Independence, July 9, 1776. The Declaration gave Americans a ringing statement of what they were fighting and sacrificing for: independence and liberty.*

Throughout the thirteen colonies the Declaration was read aloud to cheering crowds. In Worcester, Massachusetts, listeners drank a toast and wished "perpetual itching and no scratching to America's enemies." Princeton, New Jersey, celebrated with "a triple volley of musketry"; Easton, Pennsylvania, with "drums beating, fifes piping, . . . and three loud huzzas"; Savannah, Georgia, with a grand parade ending in a "very solemn funeral" for King George's "political existence." In New York City crowds toppled a statue of the king, sawed off its head, and dragged off the rest to be melted down for bullets.

A few weeks later, the members of Congress signed a fine parchment copy of the Declaration of Independence. Many were still shaken by the enormous step America had taken. "There must be no pulling different ways. We must all hang together," said John Hancock, placing his bold signature at the top. "Yes," replied Benjamin Franklin, "we must all hang together. Or most assuredly we shall all hang separately."

Two

Loyalists versus Patriots

Neighbor was against Neighbor, father against son and son against father. He that would not thrust his own blade through his brother's heart was called an infamous villain.

—A CONNECTICUT LOYALIST

A Civil War

Not all Americans celebrated the Declaration of Independence. Many remained loyal to the "mother country." John Adams estimated that about one-third of all Americans sided with Britain, one-third with independence, and a "middle third . . . were rather lukewarm," favoring one side and then the other, depending on who seemed to be on top.

No one knows for sure how accurate that estimate was. But it is certain that Americans were deeply divided. In fact, many historians call the Revolutionary War America's first civil war—a conflict that turned friends into enemies and pitted brother against brother, father against son.

Colonists loyal to Britain discuss the troubling upheavals of 1776.

Patriot and Loyalist Views

Americans who supported the Revolution called themselves Patriots. Their enemies gave them the name Whigs, from "Whiggamore," a Scottish raider or thief. Patriots came from every colony, from all classes and professions. They were united in their hatred of what they saw as tyranny and in their demand for liberty. And they were convinced that America had the will and power to win its fight. "Freemen contending for liberty on their own ground," wrote one young Patriot in 1776, "are superior to any slavish mercenary [hired soldier] on earth."

Franklin Family Feuds

The American Revolution divided friends and families, sometimes forever. Among them was the family of Benjamin Franklin. The famous scientist, inventor, writer, printer, and statesman was nearly seventy when the war began. Franklin had spent several years in England as an agent representing colonial interests. Through his influence with British government leaders, he had obtained an important colonial post for his son, William, as royal governor of New Jersey.

In 1775, returning home from an overseas mission, Franklin heard the news of the Battles of Lexington and Concord. "Has William resigned?" he asked. The answer was no. Benjamin Franklin would become one of the greatest champions of American independence, while his son would remain loyal to Britain.

The Continental Congress had William Franklin arrested and imprisoned for two years. After his release he organized a group of Loyalists to fight Continental forces in New Jersey and Connecticut. Meanwhile, *his* son, William Temple Franklin, worked for the Patriots.

After the Revolution William and William Temple quarreled bitterly and never spoke again. Benjamin and William also parted ways forever. A few years before his death in 1790, Benjamin wrote in a letter to William, "Nothing . . . ever hurt me so much . . . as to find myself deserted in my old Age by my only Son; and, not only deserted, but to find him taking up Arms against me in a Cause, wherein my good Fame, Fortune, and Life were all at stake."

PATRIOTS MAINTAINED THAT IT WAS BRITAIN'S UNREASONABLE, EXTREME ACTIONS THAT FORCED THEM TO DECLARE INDEPENDENCE. IN THIS MAY 1776 SPEECH, A FARMER FROM PHILADELPHIA OUTLINES THE REASONS HE AND OTHER REVOLUTIONARIES TOOK UP ARMS IN THE PATRIOT CAUSE.

MY FRIENDS AND COUNTRYMEN—I have observed that some of you are a little surprised that I, with so many inducements as I have to remain at home, should have resolved to quit my family, and my farm for the fatigues and dangers of war. I mean [intend that] you should be perfectly satisfied as to my motives. I am an American: and am determined to be free. I was born free: and have never forfeited my birthright. . . . I will part with my life sooner than my liberty; for I perfer an honorable death to the miserable and despicable existence of a slave. . . .

Let no one therefore wonder if, of all earthly benefits my Creator hath bestowed on me, I do most esteem my liberty. . . . [Tyranny], like a devouring cancer, the longer it is let alone, . . . the faster and deeper it will root itself into the frame, until it gnaws out the very life of the body. . . . The claims therefore of the British parliament of a power to bind us in all cases whatsoever; . . . when we have no voice in the legislation nor constitutional power allowed us to check their most violent proceedings, are not of the nature of government, but in the true and strict sense of the word tyranny.

What have we done? when alarmed, ere [before] we had yet rested from the toils of the last war, by new unconstitutional demands of revenue, we asserted our rights and petitioned for justice. Was this a crime? as unconstitutional statutes of different forms were repeatedly enacted, we repeated our petitions for redress [relief]; was this a crime? we suffered ourselves to be insulted by the introduction of an armed force to dragoon [force] us into obedience. . . : was this a crime?. . . nor did we once lift the sword even in our defence, until provoked to it by a wanton [merciless] commencement of hostilities on their part; what then have we done to merit such cruel proceedings? my friends, I am firmly persuaded, that no truth will appear in future history, with more glaring evidence, than that the whole mass of guilt contracted by this unnatural war lieth at the door of [Britain]; and so that, not only all future generations of men, but the Great Judge of all the earth, will finally condemn their measures as a scene of tyranny and murder.

Americans who remained loyal to Britain called themselves Loyalists. The Patriots labeled them Tories, from an Irish slang word for "outlaw." The Loyalists, too, came from every walk of life—rich and poor, judge and farmer, doctor and bricklayer. Some were newly arrived emigrants with close ties to the mother country. Some were merchants or seamen dependent on British trade or officeholders appointed by the British government. Loyalists lived in every colony, with the largest number in New York and in the lower South, especially Georgia and North Carolina.

MANY LOYALISTS BELIEVED THAT AMERICA HAD NO CHANCE AGAINST THE MILITARY MIGHT OF BRITAIN. IN 1777 JACOB DUCHÉ, A WELL-KNOWN PHILADELPHIA CLERGYMAN, WROTE TO GEORGE WASHINGTON, URGING HIM TO GIVE UP THE HOPELESS FIGHT. WASHINGTON GAVE THE LETTER TO THE CONTINENTAL CONGRESS, WHICH DISTRIBUTED COPIES THROUGHOUT THE STATES. PATRIOTS WERE OUTRAGED, AND DUCHÉ WAS FORCED TO LEAVE THE COUNTRY.

Philadelphia October 8th, 1777

Sir, . . . All the world must be convinced that you engaged in the service of your country from motives perfectly disinterested [unselfish]. . . . But had you? could you have had the least idea of matters being carried to such a dangerous extremity? . . .

Take an impartial view of the present Congress. What can you expect from them? Your feelings must be greatly hurt by the representation from your native province. . . . Oh my dear Sir! What a sad contrast! Characters now present themselves whose minds can never mingle with your own. . . .

As to those of my own province, some of them are so obscure, that their very names have never met my ears before, and others have only been distinguished for the weakness of their understandings and the violence of their tempers. . . .

After this view of Congress, turn to the Army. The whole world knows that its very existence depends upon you, that your death or Captivity disperses it in a moment. . . . Can you have the least confidence in a set of undisciplined men and officers, many of whom have been taken from the lowest of the people, without principle, without courage? Take away those that surround your person, how very few are there that you can ask to sit at your table?

Turn to your little Navy—of that little, what is left? . . . And now, where are your Resources? O my dear Sir, how sadly have you been abused. . . !

Your penetrating eye needs not more explicit language to discern my meaning. With that prudence and delicacy, therefore, of which I know you possessed, represent to Congress the indispensable necessity of rescinding [taking back] the hasty and ill-advised declaration of independency. Recommend (and you have an undoubted right to recommend) an immediate cessation of hostilities. . . . Millions will bless the hero, that left the field of war, to decide this most important contest with the weapons of wisdom and humanity. . . .

Your obedient & sincere friend & servant,
Jacob Duché

Just like the Patriots, most Loyalists opposed "taxation without representation" and resented Parliament's heavy-handed rule. But to these Americans, armed revolt was an even greater evil. Revolution was treason, a terrible crime. It had been provoked, Loyalists believed, by ambitious rebels whose real goal was a complete breakdown of law and order. Henry Caner of Boston argued that "Anarchy [lawlessness], & Violence, & all this flame [are] kindled & kept alive by about 1/2 dozen men of bad principles & morals." To the Reverend Richard Mansfield of Connecticut, it was obvious that the efforts of Patriot leaders "proceeded not from a Fear of the Loss of Liberty, but from a Lust of Power."

The Price of Loyalty

According to a favorite Patriot saying, a Tory was "a thing whose head is in England, whose body is in America, and whose neck needs stretching." These "infamous betrayers of their country" were regarded as a serious threat to the Revolution. Scattered throughout the colonies, they could easily spy or scout for the British and provide them with food and other supplies. Tens of thousands of Loyalists fought for Britain in regiments with names such as the Loyal Americans, the Pennsylvania Loyalists, and the Tory Rangers.

Before the fighting even began, Patriots took steps to identify Loyalists. Local governments ordered all citizens to sign an oath of loyalty to Congress. Committees of Safety were organized to administer the oath and to root out anyone secretly sid-

Many Connecticut Loyalists were locked up at a converted copper mine known as Newgate Prison. There they were held under horrible conditions in dark underground caverns, which were below the large building shown left of center in this drawing.

ing with the enemy. Committee members spied on their neighbors, listening in on conversations and reading private mail.

At first, the treatment of suspected Loyalists was fairly mild. Those who were caught criticizing Congress or praising the king might be forced to issue a public apology. One Georgia Loyalist was drummed through the streets before a laughing crowd, while a Boston man had to sit on a block of ice to "cool his loyalty." Sometimes Patriots broke the windows of Loyalists' homes or shops or blocked their chimneys to "smoke them out."

As the war continued and hatred on both sides deepened, punishments grew harsher. The Committees of Safety fined Loyalists and organized boycotts of their businesses. Many states passed laws banishing Loyalists and confiscating (taking away) all their property. Some were beaten, some thrown in jail. In New York a mob smashed the printing presses of a Loyalist newspaper and imprisoned the printers at a public inn. There, said one sympathizer, "every low-lived wretch for ten miles around . . . had free liberty to enter their apartments at pleasure and to treat them with the vilest language."

Sixteen-year-old Walter Bates of Darien, Connecticut, was whipped for refusing to lead the local Committee of Safety to his brother, who was hiding out after aiding the British. "The committee proposed many means to extort a confession from me," he later wrote. "The most terrifying was that of confining me to a log on the carriage in the Saw mill and let the saw cut me in two." Despite the threats, Walter refused to talk, and the Patriots finally gave up and released him.

Calamities of War

One of the most brutal means of punishing Loyalists was tarring and feathering. A victim was stripped, covered with a layer of hot tar, and coated with feathers from a pillow or featherbed. Then he might be ridden through town in a cart or on a wooden fence rail. It took weeks for victims of tarring and feathering to recover. Often their burned skin came off in strips, leaving them scarred for life.

"We had some Grand Toory Rides in this City this week," wrote Peter Elting of New York. "Several of them were handeld verry Roughly Being Caried trugh [through] the streets on Rails, there Clooths tore from there backs." In Hartford, Connecticut, reported a local newspaper, Dr. Joseph Clarke was seized by a mob, tarred and feathered, and

> carried upon a Rail about the Parish, under which Cruelty he several Times fainted. When dismissed by his Tormenters and examined, . . . he was found to be injured in a Manner unfit for Description in a Newspaper. The Doctor [who treated him] was menaced with the same Treatment for his Humanity to the Sufferer.

Such rough and lawless actions sometimes had an unintended result, turning undecided Americans into committed Loyalists. "I believe that committees thro' their severity have made a great many Tories," observed one New York Loyalist, "for it is natural when a man is hurt to kick." One example was Thomas Browne of Augusta, Georgia, who was tarred and feathered in 1775 for making fun of the Sons of Liberty. Browne's feet were so badly burned that he lost several toes. Swearing vengeance, he went on to lead Loyalist raids in Florida and Georgia.

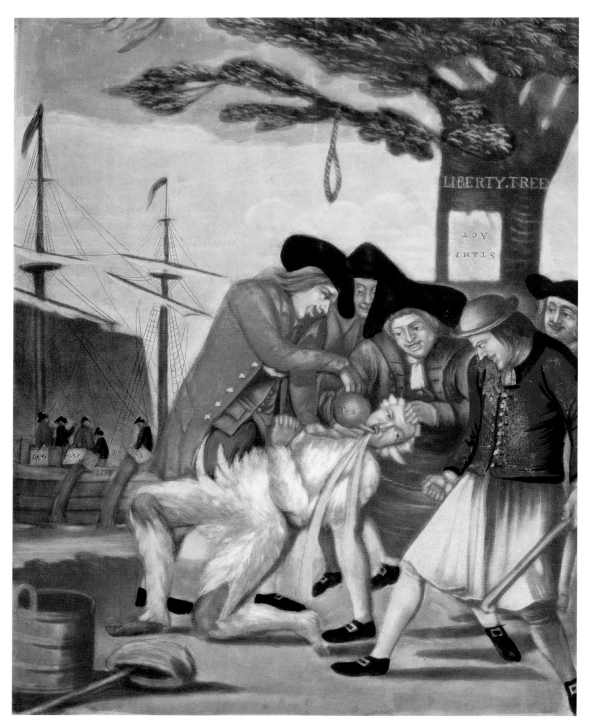

The first American tarred and feathered for loyalty to Britain was Boston tax collector John Malcolm. In this British cartoon condemning the action, some Patriots are forcing the Loyalist to drink a bowl of tea, while in the background others dump tea into Boston Harbor.

TENS OF THOUSANDS OF LOYALISTS LEFT AMERICA DURING THE REVOLUTIONARY WAR, SOME BANISHED BY THEIR STATE OR LOCAL GOVERNMENT, OTHERS DRIVEN AWAY BY THE THREAT OF PERSECUTION. AMONG THE REFUGEES WAS ANN HULTON. ANN LIVED WITH HER BROTHER, HENRY, A CUSTOMS OFFICIAL IN BOSTON, UNTIL LATE 1775, WHEN SHE SAILED FOR ENGLAND. IN THIS LETTER TO A FRIEND IN LIVERPOOL, SHE DESCRIBES SOME OF THE SCENES OF VIOLENCE THAT WERE MAKING BOSTON A DANGEROUS PLACE FOR ITS LOYALIST CITIZENS.

January 31st 1774

[Dear Madam]

You will perhaps expect me to give you some Account of the State of Boston & late proceedings here but really the times are too bad & the Scenes too shocking for me to describe. . . .

The most shocking cruelty was exercised a few Nights ago, upon a poor Old Man. . . . A quarrel was picked with him, he was afterward taken, & Tarrd, & featherd. Theres no Law that knows a punishment for the greatest Crimes beyond what this is, of cruel torture. And this instance exceeds any other before it. He was stript Stark naked, one of the severest cold nights this Winter, his body coverd all over with Tar, then with feathers, his arm dislocated in tearing off his cloaths, he was dragged in a Cart with thousands attending, some beating him with clubs & Knocking him out of the Cart, then in again. They gave him several severe whipings, at different parts of the Town. This Spectacle of horror & sportive cruelty was exhibited for about five hours.

. . . .When under Torture they demanded of him to curse his Masters The King: Governor &c [etc.] which they coud not make him do, but he still cried, Curse all Traitors. They brought him to the Gallows & put a rope about his neck saying they woud hang him. He said he wishd they woud, but that they coud not for God was above the Devil. The Doctors say that it is imposible this poor creature can live. They say his flesh comes off his back in Stakes [strips]. . . .

These few instances amongst many serve to shew the abject [low] State of Government & the licentiousness [lack of control] & barbarism of the times. There's no Majestrate [judge] that dare or will act to suppress the outrages. No person is secure. . . .

We are under no apprehension [fear] at present on our own Account but we can't look upon our Safety, secure for Long.

[A. Hulton]

Americans on both sides paid a terrible price in the Revolutionary War, with friendships and families shattered; homes, property, and lives lost. "The worst which can happen is [about] to fall on the last bleak mountain of America," Gouverneur Morris, a devoted Patriot, wrote to his Loyalist mother in 1776. "What may be the event [outcome] of the present war, it is not in man to determine. Great revolutions of empire are seldom achieved without much human calamity."

Three

Yankee Doodle on Land and Sea

The horses attached to our cannon were without shoes, and when passing over the ice they would slide in every direction. . . . Our men, too, were without shoes or other comfortable clothing; and as traces of our march towards Princeton, the ground was literally marked with the blood of the soldiers' feet.

—A CONTINENTAL SOLDIER, JANUARY 1777

"Times That Try Men's Souls"

When George Washington got his first look at the Continental troops camped outside Boston in June 1775, he found them "an exceeding dirty and nasty people." The men drank, gambled, and quarreled. They swore at their officers and generally did whatever they pleased. Washington cracked down. He replaced the camp's makeshift tents and huts with military barracks, posted long lists of regulations, and ordered fines and lashings for any man who broke the rules.

This painting presents a romanticized view of the Continentals, who soldiered on through grim conditions that included severe cold, short rations, ragged uniforms, and irregular pay.

THE REVEREND WILLIAM EMERSON OF CONCORD WAS A FREQUENT VISITOR TO THE AMERICAN CAMP OUTSIDE BOSTON. HE WAS IMPRESSED WITH THE NEW ORDER THAT GENERAL WASHINGTON BROUGHT TO THE CONTINENTAL ARMY. IN THIS LETTER TO HIS WIFE, THE CLERGYMAN DESCRIBES THE DISMAL CONDITIONS WASHINGTON FOUND AND THE STEPS HE TOOK TO CORRECT THEM.

July 17, 1775

. . . 'Tis also very diverting to walk among the camps. They are as different in their form as the owners are in their dress; and every tent is a portraiture of ye temper and taste of ye persons that incamp in it. Some are made of boards, some of sailcloth, and some partly of one and partly of the other. Others are made of stone and turf, and others again of Birch and other brush. Some are thrown up in a hurry and look as if they could not help it—mere necessity—others are curiously wrought with doors and windows done with wreaths and withes [twigs] in the manner of a basket. Some are your proper tents . . . , and look like ye regular camp of the enemy. These are the Rhode-islanders, who are furnished with tent equipage from among ourselves and every thing in the most exact English taste. However I think that the great variety of the American camp is upon the whole, rather a beauty than a blemish to the army. . . .

There is great overturning in camp, as to order and regularity. New lords new laws. The Generals Washington and [Charles] Lee are upon the lines every day. New orders from his Excellency [Washington] are read to the respective regiments every morning after prayers. The strictest government is taking place, and great distinction is made between officers and soldiers. Everyone is made to know his place and keep in it, or be tied up and receive . . . thirty or forty lashes according to his crime. Thousands are at work every day from four till eleven o'clock in the morning. It is surprising how much work has been done.

Gradually, Washington imposed order. By March 1776 he had built an army strong enough to force the British to evacuate Boston. But the Continentals still had a long way to go, and the enemy was far from finished.

In June hundreds of British ships carrying men and supplies began pouring into New York harbor. It was the largest invasion force Britain had ever sent overseas—more than 30,000 soldiers, including Redcoats and German mercenaries (hired soldiers) called Hessians. On August 27 the British and Hessian forces met 8,000 Continentals in the Battle of Long Island and overwhelmed them.

The Americans fell back. The British followed. For the next four months, Washington's army made a fighting retreat through New York and New Jersey, then across the Delaware River into Pennsylvania. Thomas Paine was traveling with the Continentals. In December he began a series of essays called *The Crisis.*

> These are the times that try men's souls. The summer soldier and the sunshine patriot will, in this crisis, shrink from the service of their country; but he that stands it *now* deserves the love and thanks of man and woman. Tyranny, like hell, is not easily conquered; yet we have this consolation with us, that the harder the conflict, the more glorious the triumph.

Washington had Paine's stirring words read to his troops. The men were weak and discouraged, ragged and hungry. Deaths, desertions, and expired enlistments had reduced their number to around five thousand. Many of the remaining soldiers planned to go home on New Year's Eve, when their enlistments expired.

Only a desperate move could save the Patriot cause.

On Christmas night 1776 Washington's army boarded small wooden boats and rowed silently across the Delaware. "It was as severe a night as I ever saw," recalled Captain Thomas Rodney. "The frost was sharp, the current difficult to stem, the ice increasing, the wind high." By 3 A.M. all the men were safely ashore. In a driving sleet storm, they jogged nine miles to the British garrison at Trenton, New Jersey. The Americans arrived just after dawn. The troops manning the post were still sleeping off their Christmas dinner. The assault was a complete surprise and a stunning victory.

These officers and soldiers belong to a battalion of Hessians—Germans hired to fight for the British during the Revolution. Americans surprised and defeated a large force of Hessians in the Battle of Trenton.

HENRY KNOX WAS A YOUNG BOOKSTORE OWNER WHO TAUGHT HIMSELF ABOUT ARTILLERY BY READING THE BOOKS IN HIS BOSTON SHOP. IN EARLY 1775 KNOX HAD EARNED WASHINGTON'S RESPECT AND GRATITUDE BY TRANSPORTING THE CANNONS CAPTURED AT FORT TICONDEROGA THREE HUNDRED MILES TO END THE SIEGE OF BOSTON. THE SELF-TAUGHT GUNNERY EXPERT ALSO MADE IMPORTANT CONTRIBUTIONS AT THE BATTLE OF TRENTON. IN THIS LETTER TO HIS WIFE, LUCY, KNOX DESCRIBES THAT PATRIOT VICTORY, WHICH EARNED HIM A PROMOTION TO BRIGADIER GENERAL.

Dec. 28, 1776, near 12 o'clock

My dearly beloved friend,—You will before this have heard of our success on the morning of the 26th. . . .

Our intelligence agreed that the force of the enemy in Trenton was from two to three thousand, with about six field cannon, and that they were pretty secure in their situation, and that they were Hessians,—no British troops. A hardy design was formed of attacking the town by storm. Accordingly a part of the army, consisting of about 2,500 or 3,000, passed the river on Christmas night, with almost infinite difficulty, with eighteen field-pieces [cannons]. The floating ice in the river made the labor almost incredible. However, perseverance accomplished what at first seemed impossible. About two o'clock the troops were all on the Jersey side; we then were about nine miles from the object. The night was cold and stormy; it hailed with great violence; the troops marched with the most profound silence and good order.

They arrived by two routes at the same time, about half an hour after daylight, within one mile of the town. . . . Here succeeded a scene of war of which I had often conceived, but never saw before. The hurry, fright, and confusion of the enemy was [not] unlike that which will be when the last trump [trumpet] shall sound. They endeavored to form in streets, the heads of which we had previously the possession of with cannon and howitzers [short cannons]; these, in the twinkling of an eye, cleared the streets. . . . Finally they were driven through the town into an open plain beyond. . . . The poor fellows after they were formed on the plain saw themselves completely surrounded. . . . The Hessians . . . were obliged to surrender upon the spot, with all their artillery. . . .

His Excellency the General has done me the unmerited great honor of thanking me in public orders in terms strong and polite. This I should blush to mention to any other than to you, my dear Lucy.

A few days later, in another surprise attack, the Continental army captured Princeton. The British pulled back, abandoning most of the lands they had occupied in New Jersey. "The enemy have fled before us in the greatest panic that ever was known," Thomas Rodney exulted. "Never were men in higher spirits than our whole army is."

Philadelphia Falls

After their victories at Trenton and Princeton, the Continentals spent the winter camped at Morristown, New Jersey. The following spring brought fresh recruits. Thousands had been lured by Congress's offer of twenty dollars and one hundred acres of land to all who enlisted for three years. Joseph Plumb Martin, a sixteen-year-old farm boy from Massachusetts, was one of the thousands who signed up, swayed by

> the general opinion of the people . . . that the war would not continue three years longer; what reasons they had for making such conjectures [guesses] I cannot imagine, but so it was. Perhaps it was their wish that it *might* be so, induced them to think that it *would* be so.

The British, too, were convinced that the war was nearly at an end. In fact, they planned to make 1777 the year of the knockout blow. British forces would launch a three-pronged attack. One army, led by General John Burgoyne, would march south from Canada along the Hudson River to attack Albany, New York. A smaller force would follow the Mohawk River and approach Albany from the west. The third British army, under General William Howe, would move up the Hudson from New York City. When the three forces met, the rebellious colonies would be cut in half.

It was a foolproof plan—and it went terribly wrong. The first step toward disaster was Howe's decision to make a side trip and capture the rebel capital at Philadelphia. Washington's army raced to stop him. At Brandywine Creek, about twenty-five miles south of Philadelphia, the two forces fought a furious battle that

Clinton's Secret Message

In August 1777 General Henry Clinton sent General John Burgoyne a letter *(below left)* that seemed to contain a jumble of military small talk. But when Burgoyne covered the sheet with an hourglass-shaped cutout *(below right)*, he could read the disturbing news: General Howe had gone to Philadelphia, and his troops would not be reinforcing Burgoyne's attack on Albany.

Here's how the decoded message read:

Sir W. Howe is gone to the Chesapeak bay with the greatest part of his army. I hear he is landed but am not certain. I am left to command here with too small a force to make any effectual diversion in your favour I shall try something at any rate. It may be of use to you. I own to you I think Sir W.'s move just at this time the worst he could take.

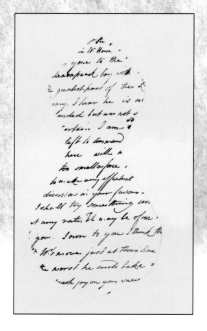

ended in an American retreat. The British marched on to Philadelphia. Meanwhile, Washington regrouped his forces. On October 4 the Americans attacked Howe's main camp at Germantown, just north of the capital. The early-morning raid so surprised the British, Joseph Plumb Martin recalled, that "they left their kettles, in which they were cooking their breakfasts, on the fires, and some of their garments were lying on the ground, which the owners had not time to put on."

It looked like the Continentals might win the day. Then, in a dense fog, two American divisions began firing at each other. Confusion led to panic, and thousands turned and ran. Germantown ended in another British victory. But the fact that the infant rebel army had come so close to defeating seasoned British troops left Washington's men in high spirits. And the weeks that Howe had wasted battling the stubborn Americans meant that he could not join General Burgoyne in northern New York.

A Turning Point

Burgoyne's eight thousand men had spent nearly four weeks stumbling through thick woods and marshes on their long trek toward Albany. A raiding party sent to gather supplies had been wiped out by militiamen. Next came the bad news that Howe's troops were stalled in Philadelphia. The reinforcements expected from the west had also been derailed by the Americans. Burgoyne was on his own.

Near Saratoga, New York, the British found their way blocked by six thousand Continentals under General Horatio Gates. On September 19 the armies fought one bloody battle that ended in a draw. Then, on October 7, frontiersman Daniel Morgan and his Pennsylvania riflemen kicked off the second Battle of Saratoga. "Morgan . . . poured down like a torrent from the hill," recalled a Continental colonel, "and attacked the right of the enemy." When the British retreated, Benedict Arnold spurred the attack. Galloping up and down the battle lines, the fiery general shouted encouragement "with a voice that rung clear as a trumpet." Arnold led charge after charge, until his horse was shot from under him and he fell wounded. Then the American advance faltered. Shaken and exhausted, the British fled behind defensive walls they had built at Saratoga, leaving more than six hundred dead and wounded on the battlefield.

Burgoyne's troops were surrounded, their food and ammunition nearly gone. On October 17 the British general surrendered his army.

It was the turning point of the Revolution. The victory at Saratoga proved that America had a good chance of winning its fight. That proof won the Patriots a valuable partner. France was already secretly supplying the rebels with arms and ammunition, but it had been reluctant to enter an all-out war with its ancient enemy Britain until it was certain the rebels were a serious power. After the news of Saratoga, the French were convinced. On February 6, 1778, they signed a treaty recognizing American independence and pledging to fight alongside the young nation as "good and faithful allies."

Winter at Valley Forge

As Americans celebrated the victory at Saratoga, George Washington and his men were marching toward winter quarters at Valley Forge, Pennsylvania. "We arrived," wrote Joseph Plumb Martin, "a few days before Christmas. Our prospect was indeed dreary." The men were tired and hungry, and

> the greatest part were not only shirtless and barefoot, but destitute [lacking] of all other clothing except blankets. I procured [obtained] a small piece of raw cowhide and made myself a pair of moccasins. . . . The hard edges so galled my ankles, while on a march, that it was with much difficulty and pain that I could wear them afterwards; but the only alternative I had was to . . . go barefoot, as hundreds of my companions had to, till they might be tracked by their blood upon the rough frozen ground.

In the bitter cold the weary soldiers cut down trees and built rough log shelters. To provide for the army, foraging parties searched the countryside for sheep, cattle, corn, flour, and other supplies. Often the foragers returned empty-handed. Then the men lived on firecake—a thin bread of flour and water cooked over a campfire—and sometimes on nothing but water.

A bedraggled rebel soldier trudges through the snow toward the Continental army's quarters at Valley Forge, Pennsylvania, in the winter of 1777–1778.

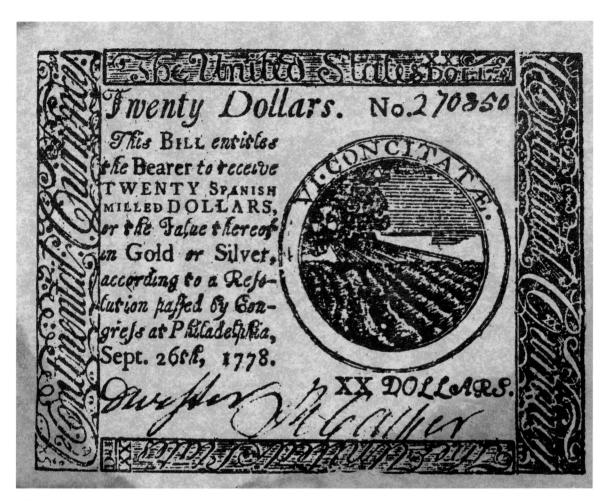

The Continental Congress printed paper money to replace the European coins used in the colonies before the war. Because of America's shaky economy, however, the value of the currency kept dropping—an item that cost 20 Continental dollars in 1776 cost more than 20,000 dollars by 1780.

Nearly 2,500 of the 11,000 men died during the four months at Valley Forge, most from smallpox, pneumonia, and other diseases. The lucky ones muddled through the cold and hunger, the filth, lice, and frostbite. Adding to the soldiers' misery was the knowledge that the year's harvest had been plentiful and the rest of America was feasting. The troops were suffering because the government's system for supplying them was hopelessly inefficient, and because many farmers and

"Yankee Doodle"

Compared with the British in their crisp scarlet uniforms, the ragged rebel army looked like country bumpkins. The Redcoats sometimes mocked the Americans with a tune called "Yankee Doodle." The song made fun of a "doodle" (fool), who put on "macaroni" (phony) airs and had trouble coordinating his marching steps. There were many different versions. One of the most popular began:

Yankee Doodle came to town
A-riding on a pony,
He stuck a feather in his hat
And called it macaroni.

Yankee Doodle keep it up,
Yankee Doodle Dandy,
Mind the music and the step
And with the girls be handy.

In time, the Americans defiantly adopted the song as their own. One of the Continental soldiers' favorite versions ended this way:

Yankee Doodle is the tune
That we all delight in;
It suits for feasts, it suits for fun,
And just as well for fightin'.

merchants hoarded their goods or even traded with the enemy rather than accept Congress's nearly worthless "Continental dollars."

A handful of foreign volunteers shared the Americans' hardships at Valley Forge. The Marquis de Lafayette, an idealistic young French nobleman who had fought bravely in the Philadelphia campaign, wrote that "the patient fortitude [strength] of officers and soldiers was a continual miracle that each moment renewed." Baron Friedrich von Steuben, a former Prussian officer, drilled the Continentals for endless hours in battlefield maneuvers. Von Steuben was a red-faced, excitable man. When the soldiers didn't perform correctly, he would launch into a stream of German, French, and English curse words that had them doubled up in laughter. But the men learned much under his skilled training, and the Continental army emerged from its hard winter at Valley Forge a more confident and disciplined fighting force than ever.

Birth of a Navy

The Revolution at sea was a David and Goliath affair. Britain was the giant, with a navy that boasted 270 ships in 1775. About half of these were ships of the line—huge, heavy warships with sixty-four or more cannons, capable of hurling a half ton of metal in one mighty blast.

America started out with no naval force at all. In October 1775 Congress voted to create a navy, beginning with two small, swift merchant ships outfitted with guns. Later, money was raised to build thirteen frigates—medium-size ships with up to forty-four guns. Several colonies also had their own small navies.

The Continental navy was never large enough to challenge the British in full battle. Instead, it waged war one ship at a time. The hero of these small but deadly skirmishes was John Paul Jones. The Scottish-born captain captured or sank nearly a hundred enemy warships and trading vessels and threw Britain into an uproar with daring raids on ports all along the enemy's coasts. In 1779, commanding the *Bonhomme Richard,* Jones scored the Continental navy's greatest triumph, capturing the fifty-gun British warship the *Serapis.* During the four-hour sea battle, Jones reportedly answered the British call to surrender with a defiant line that would become famous: "I have not yet begun to fight!"

The four-hour engagement between America's converted merchant ship Bonhomme Richard *(left) and the British warship* Serapis *in September 1779 was the greatest naval battle of the Revolution. Captain John Paul Jones and his crew triumphed, but their ship was so badly damaged that it sank two days later.*

Privateers and Prison Ships

While the Continental navy harassed and infuriated Britain, it was the privateers that inflicted the greatest damage on enemy shipping. Privateering was legalized piracy. Owners of small, fast, armed trading vessels were granted government licenses to attack enemy ships and seize their cargo. The privateers' owners, officers, and crew divided the prize money. More than 60,000 American men and boys signed aboard privateers during the war, hoping to "serve their Country and make their Fortunes." Altogether, privateers sank or captured about six hundred British ships carrying supplies worth about eighteen million dollars, a considerable sum at the time.

American naval hero John Paul Jones. For his daring exploits and skilled leadership, the dashing captain has become known as the Father of the American Navy.

FIFTEEN-YEAR-OLD JOHN GREENWOOD ENLISTED AS A FIFER WITH A BOSTON REGIMENT IN 1775 AND SERVED DURING THE BATTLES OF BUNKER HILL, QUEBEC, AND TRENTON. AFTER HIS ENLISTMENT EXPIRED, GREENWOOD SIGNED ABOARD SEVERAL PRIVATEERS. HERE HE DESCRIBES HIS ADVENTURES IN 1779 ABOARD THE *TARTAR*, A PRIVATEER OUT OF BOSTON.

We had orders to cruise off New York, but unfortunately we were blown by a gale of wind into the Gulf Stream. The wind, being at northeast, was directly against the current, thus making a terrible cross sea which hove up mountains high. It continued to blow six days and nights and the pumps were kept constantly at work, for, with 4 feet of water in the hold and the ship so old and crazy, we expected to go to the bottom every moment. . . .

Off the island of Jamaica we very soon took three prizes and carried them up to Port-au-Prince in Hispaniola, into which place, after refitting our ship and proceeding to Jamaica again, we presently brought some more prizes. Our ship was so old, crazy, and leaky that we were obliged to nail strips of rawhide over the seams of her upper works in order to keep the oakum in place. For six months we continued cruising round the island of Jamaica, landing sometimes twice a week, in fact as often as we felt inclined to do so, to procure fresh provisions such as hogs, sheep, and poultry. This was in spite of the great vigilance and superiority of the British cruisers, for our vessel was always disguised in such a manner that they could never tell where we were, from any information given them from the shore. At times her sides would be painted black or yellow or red, occasionally we would run our guns in, . . . and appear like a ship in distress; and we had a number of such maneuvers for deception. . . .

We went near the shore, behind a cape or point of land not far from a place called, I think, Black River, in the island of Jamaica, while our ship kept off some distance with British colors flying. As the drogers [trade ships] came round the point and saw us they would haul off to our ship for protection, thinking it was an English vessel, so that in a few days we took eleven sail of vessels, brigs, sloops, and one ship of eighteen guns, and carried them all into Port-au-Prince.

Life aboard a privateer was hard and risky. The seaman's day was a dull routine of repetitive chores, foul meals, and sleep in crowded, smelly quarters. Punctuating the long stretches of boredom were intervals of excitement and danger—storms and high seas, battles with enemy vessels, cannonballs flying and bayonets flashing.

One of the greatest dangers was capture. While soldiers captured on land often were traded for enemy prisoners of war, the British sent captured privateersmen to prison ships for the duration. The worst was the *Jersey*, anchored in New York's East River. Thousands of prisoners crowded in this floating dungeon's dark, dirty, stifling holds. The food was scarce, and rats and other pests spread diseases. Thomas Dring of Connecticut, imprisoned for five months on the *Jersey*, was shocked at his first sight of the "shrunken and decayed" captives, their faces "covered with dirt and filth, their long hair and beards matted and foul." The hardest times, Dring recalled, were the long nights when

> silence was a stranger to our dark abode. The groans of the sick and dying; the curses poured out by weary and exhausted men upon our inhuman keepers; the restlessness caused by the suffocating heat and the confined and poisonous air; mingled with the wild and incoherent ravings of delirium, were the sounds, which every night were raised around us.

Nearly 11,000 privateersmen died on the *Jersey* and other prison ships—more than all the Americans killed on Revolutionary battlefields.

Four

Americans All

If there be an object truly ridiculous in nature, it is an
American patriot signing resolutions of independence with
the one hand, and with the other brandishing a whip
over his affrighted slaves.

—ENGLISHMAN THOMAS DAY, 1776

"Liberty for Slaves"

Most of the Americans who shivered at Valley Forge and shipped out on privateers were white men. But America itself was a blend of men, women, and children; white, black, and Native American; free and unfree.

In 1776 one of every five Americans was black. Of these, more than 90 percent were slaves. There were slaves in every colony, but most lived in the South, working as household servants or laboring in tobacco, cotton, or sugar plantation fields.

African Americans greeted the Revolution with excitement and hope. A war for political liberty held the promise of personal freedom, too. The stirring words of the Declaration of Independence had special significance for an enslaved people:

We hold these Truths to be self-evident, that all Men are created equal, that they are endowed by their Creator with certain unalienable Rights, that among these are Life, Liberty, and the pursuit of Happiness.

THE REVOLUTIONARY CRY FOR LIBERTY TOUCHED THE HEARTS AND MINDS OF AMERICAN SLAVES. IN APRIL 1773 FOUR SLAVES FROM MASSACHUSETTS SENT THIS LETTER TO THEIR TOWN'S REPRESENTATIVE IN THE COLONIAL LEGISLATURE, ASKING FOR THE RIGHT TO WORK FOR THEMSELVES ONE DAY A WEEK SO THEY MIGHT SAVE ENOUGH MONEY TO BUY THEIR FREEDOM. THEIR REQUEST WAS DENIED. SLAVERY WAS ABOLISHED IN SEVERAL MASSACHUSETTS TOWNS IN 1776 AND THROUGHOUT THE STATE IN 1783.

BOSTON, April 20th, 1773

SIR, The efforts made by the legislative of this province in their last sessions to free themselves from slavery, gave us, who are in that deplorable state, a high degree of satisfaction. We expect great things from men who have made such a noble stand against the designs of their fellow-men to enslave them. We cannot but wish and hope Sir, that you will have the same grand object, we mean civil and religious liberty, in view in your next session. The divine spirit of freedom, seems to fire every humane breast on this continent, except such as are bribed to assist in executing the execrable [detestable] plan. . . .

Even the Spaniards, who have not those sublime ideas of freedom that English men

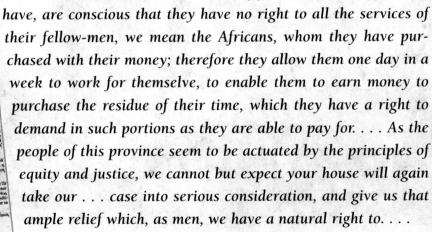

have, are conscious that they have no right to all the services of their fellow-men, we mean the Africans, whom they have purchased with their money; therefore they allow them one day in a week to work for themselve, to enable them to earn money to purchase the residue of their time, which they have a right to demand in such portions as they are able to pay for. . . . As the people of this province seem to be actuated by the principles of equity and justice, we cannot but expect your house will again take our . . . case into serious consideration, and give us that ample relief which, as men, we have a natural right to. . . .

Peter Bestes, Sambo Freeman, Felix Holbrook, Chester Joie

But the signers of the Declaration meant all *white* men. In fact, one of the changes they made to Thomas Jefferson's original Declaration was to take out a section condemning the slave trade. One-third of the signers, including Jefferson himself, were slaveholders. So were many other Patriot leaders. This discouraging fact convinced many slaves that their best chance for freedom lay with Britain. During the war, thousands fled from southern plantations to join the British forces. Escaped slaves worked as servants and laborers in British army camps and fought with British regiments. One group from Virginia fought in an all-black regiment with the words "Liberty for Slaves" stitched on their uniforms.

Other African Americans adopted the Patriot cause. At first, the Continental army excluded them, mainly because slaveholders feared that arming slaves would lead to a revolt. That policy changed after 1777, as the army became increasingly desperate for recruits. Colonies began enlisting African-American men, including slaves, who were sometimes sent as substitutes for their owners, sometimes promised their freedom in return for faithful service.

As many as 5,000 of the 30,000 men who served in the Continental army were black. For the most part, whites and blacks served side by side. "No Regiment is to be seen," observed one Hessian officer, "in which there are not Negroes in abundance; and among them are able-

James Armistead Lafayette was born a slave in Virginia and won his freedom through his services as a double agent for the Continental army.

Europeans for America

The American Revolution's ideals of liberty and equality inspired a number of European volunteers. We have already met Prussian drillmaster Baron Friedrich von Steuben and the young Marquis de Lafayette. Another Frenchman who joined the cause was the Chevalier de Mauduit du Plessis, a military engineer. In 1777 du Plessis was given the job of strengthening New Jersey's Fort Mercer. Observing that the fort was too large for its four-hundred-man garrison to defend, he built a new inside wall. A month later, two thousand Hessians attacked. They stormed the fort's outer walls, only to find themselves trapped in an empty enclosure, facing du Plessis's stout new wall—and at the mercy of the Americans massed above.

Other European volunteers came from Denmark, Sweden, Hungary, Germany, and Poland. Two outstanding Polish officers were Casimir Pulaski and Thaddeus Kosciuszko. Pulaski, a skilled cavalry officer, created the Continental army's first horseback unit. He was fatally wounded in 1779 while leading a charge against the British at Savannah, Georgia. Kosciuszko, a military engineer, designed a series of strong and elaborate fortifications for the Patriots at the Battle of Saratoga, helping to bring about the American victory.

Polish military engineer Thaddeus Kosciuszko designed the Americans' fortifications at the Battle of Saratoga and in defense of West Point, on the Hudson River in New York.

bodied, strong, and brave fellows." Black Patriots also served in the Continental navy and aboard privateers.

Some of the most daring worked as spies. James Armistead was a slave in Virginia who received his master's permission to serve under the Marquis de Lafayette. Under the Marquis's instructions, he became a double agent, posing as a runaway and pretending to spy for the British. All the while he was actually gathering valuable military information for the Americans. After the war Lafayette told the Virginia legislature that Armistead had done "essential service. . . . His intelligence from the enemy's camp were industriously collected and more faithfully delivered." The state granted the intrepid slave his freedom, and he adopted the Frenchman's last name, becoming known as James Armistead Lafayette.

Women at War

Like American men, the women of the colonies were divided by the Revolution. Some were Loyalists, some equally devoted Patriots. Whatever their politics, women found their lives dramatically altered by war.

When soldiers marched off to battle, the wives and daughters they left behind often took over the job of running the family farm or business. Many Patriot women also took an active role in supporting the struggle for liberty. They organized boycotts of British goods and Loyalist businesses. They wove cloth and made clothing and blankets for the Continental army. Esther

Flora MacDonald emigrated from Scotland to North Carolina in 1774. Her husband and two of her sons fought in a Loyalist regiment, and Flora herself became a heroine of the Loyalist cause.

Reed, the wife of a member of Washington's staff, organized the Association, a group of Philadelphia women who collected donations for the army. When Reed died in 1780, Benjamin Franklin's daughter, Sarah, continued her work. The money raised by the Association was used to buy linen, made into more than two thousand shirts for American soldiers.

LIKE MANY AMERICAN WOMEN, ABIGAIL ADAMS RAN THE HOUSEHOLD, RAISED THE CHILDREN, AND MANAGED THE FAMILY BUSINESS WHEN WAR DUTIES CALLED HER HUSBAND, JOHN, FROM HOME. HER LETTERS TO JOHN REVEAL A LIVELY, INTELLIGENT WOMAN WITH A KEEN INTEREST IN THE ISSUES OF THE TIMES. HERE ABIGAIL (WHO OFTEN SIGNED HER LETTERS "PORTIA," AFTER THE FEARLESS HEROINE OF ONE OF WILLIAM SHAKESPEARE'S PLAYS) DESCRIBES HOW A GROUP OF BOSTON WOMEN DEALT WITH A PROFITEER—A MERCHANT WHO TOOK ADVANTAGE OF THE CRISIS TO SELL HIS GOODS AT INFLATED PRICES.

July 31 [1777]

I have nothing new to entertain you with, unless it is an account of a new Set of Mobility [mob] which have lately taken the lead in Boston. You must know that there is a great Scarcity of Sugar and Coffe, articles which the Female part of the State are very loth [reluctant] to give up, especially whilst they consider the Scarcity occasiond by the merchants having Secreted a large quantity. There has been much rout & Noise in the Town for Several weeks. Some Stores had been opend by a number of people and the Coffe & Sugar carried into the market and dealt out by pounds. It was rumourd that an eminent, wealthy, Stingy Merchant (who is a Batchelor) had a Hogshead [barrel] of Coffe in his Store which he refused to sell to the committee under 6 Shillings per pound. A Number of Females, some say a hundred, some say more assembled with a cart & trucks, marchd down to the Ware House & demanded the keys, which he refused to deliver, upon which one of them seazd him by his neck and tossd him into the cart. Upon his finding no quarter [mercy] he deliverd the keys, when they tipd up the cart & dischargd him, then opend the warehouse, Hoisted out the Coffe themselves, put it into the trucks and drove off.

It was reported that he had a Spanking among them, but this I believe was not true. A large concourse of Men stood amazd Silent Spectators of the whole transaction. . . .

Portia

Women writers also supported the struggle. Mercy Otis Warren wrote plays and poems mocking the Loyalists and applauding the Patriot cause. Mary Katherine Goddard published a Patriot newspaper, the *Baltimore Journal.* Most famous of all was Phillis Wheatley. A freed slave and the first important African-American writer, Wheatley wrote poems in praise of liberty. In 1775 she dedicated a poem to the new commander of American forces, ending with these verses:

> Proceed, great chief, with virtue on thy side,
> Thy every action let the goddess guide.
> A crown, a mansion, and a throne that shine,
> With gold unfading, WASHINGTON! Be thine.

Some women played an even more active role in the fight. When the British marched toward Danbury, Connecticut, in 1777, sixteen-year-old Sibyl Ludington galloped forty miles on horseback, banging on farmhouse doors to alert the militia. In a town in Virginia, another teenage girl, Betty Zane, became a heroine during an assault on the Continentals' Fort Henry. The Patriots were running low on ammunition, so Betty dashed to a nearby house, loaded a tablecloth with gunpowder, and braved a shower of bullets to drag it back to the fort's defenders. Flora MacDonald, a Scottish-born woman loyal to Britain, helped organize a Loyalist uprising at Moore's Creek, North Carolina, in 1776. When Flora was sent back to Scotland, her ship was attacked by a privateer, and she rallied the sailors to make a spirited resistance.

Sara Osborn of New York was a camp follower—one of the hundreds of women who traveled with the Continental army, earning their keep as cooks, laundresses, seamstresses, and nurses. During one campaign, Sara

> heard the roar of the artillery for a number of days. [Her] husband was there throwing up entrenchments, and [she] cooked and carried in beef, and bread, and coffee (in a gallon pot) to the soldiers in the entrenchment. On one occasion when [she] was thus employed carrying provisions, she met General Washington who asked her if she "was not afraid of the cannonballs?" She replied, "No. . . . It would not do for the men to fight and starve, too."

A handful of women performed brave and valuable service as spies. Lydia Darragh was a fifty-two-year-old mother of nine when the British occupied Philadelphia in 1777. One evening General William Howe and his officers used Lydia's large back room for a top-secret meeting. Tiptoeing to a closet next to the room, she listened in and learned that the British were planning an attack on the Continental camp. The next morning Lydia made her way behind the American lines. Washington's men were waiting in force when the British marched out from Philadelphia—and laughing when the enemy turned tail and retreated back to the city.

Frontiers Aflame

Most Native Americans sided with Britain in the Revolutionary War. For years American settlers had been pushing west into their lands, and the Indians hoped that a British victory would stop them. A smaller number of Indians remained neutral or supported the Patriots.

Washington planned to use the Patriots' Indian allies "as scouts and light troops, mixed with our own Parties." The British pledged to "loose the savages against the miserable Rebels in order to impose a reign of terror on the frontiers." In the 1770s the American frontier stretched all the way from western Maine (then part of Massachusetts) to western Georgia, with some parts only a few hundred miles from the Atlantic coast. Throughout the war bloody raids, skirmishes, and massacres kept this vast region in constant turmoil.

"The flames of conflagrated [burning] houses and barns soon announced to the other little towns the certainty of their country's defeat," wrote Hector St. John Crèvecoeur. The French-born Patriot was describing a July 1778 attack by 1,200 Indians and Loyalists on frontier settlements in northeastern Pennsylvania's Wyoming Valley. The attackers killed and scalped 300 militiamen. Then, reported the New York *Journal,*

> they proceeded to the destruction of every building and improvement . . . that came within their reach [throughout] all these flourishing settlements. . . . When these miscreants [criminals] had destroyed the other improvements, they proceeded to

destroy the crops . . . letting in the cattle and horses to the corn, and cutting up as much as they could of what was left. Great numbers of cattle they shot and destroyed.

After devastating the Wyoming Valley, the raiders continued their attacks all along the New York-Pennsylvania frontier. In November a group led by Mohawk chief Joseph Brant struck at Cherry Valley, west of Albany. Brant was a committed Loyalist who had persuaded most of the six nations of the Iroquois League to side with Britain. He was known for showing mercy to innocent settlers, but this time he lost control of his warriors. The men slaughtered and horribly mutilated more than thirty settlers, mostly women and children.

Determined to prevent further attacks, Washington authorized a full-scale invasion of Iroquois lands. In the summer of 1779, General John Sullivan led four thousand Continentals across the New York frontier. The soldiers torched Indian villages and destroyed their crops, until Sullivan could report that not "a single settlement or field of corn" was left standing. Years after the war an Iroquois leader told Washington, "When your army entered the country of the Six Nations, we called you Town Destroyer; and to this day when that name is heard our women look behind them and turn pale, and children cling close to the necks of their mothers."

Mohawk Chief Thayendanegea, known to the Americans and British as Joseph Brant

AMERICAN SETTLERS WERE SHOCKED BY STORIES OF NATIVE AMERICAN ATROCITIES, BUT THEY WERE JUST AS CAPABLE OF CRUELTY. GEORGE ROGERS CLARK WAS A PATRIOT HERO WHO LED A DARING MISSION TO CONQUER THE OLD NORTHWEST—THE REGION BETWEEN THE OHIO RIVER AND THE GREAT LAKES—FROM THE BRITISH AND THEIR INDIAN ALLIES. ON FEBRUARY 23, 1779, CLARK AND HIS MEN CAPTURED THE BRITISH FORT AT VINCENNES, IN PRESENT-DAY INDIANA, FROM LIEUTENANT GOVERNOR HENRY HAMILTON. HAMILTON WAS KNOWN AS THE "HAIRBUYER" BECAUSE HE PAID INDIANS FOR THE SCALPS OF WHITE SET-TLERS. IN HIS ACCOUNT OF CLARK'S TREATMENT OF FOUR INDIAN PRISONERS, HOWEVER, IT IS THE BRITISH COMMANDER HIMSELF WHO IS HORRIFIED.

The [prisoners] were surrounded and taken bound to the village, where being set in the street opposite the Fort they were put to death, notwithstanding a truce at that moment existed. . . .

One of them was tomahawk'd immediately. . . . Seeing by the fate of their comrade what they had to expect, the next on his left sang his death song, and was in turn tom-ahawk'd, the rest underwent the same fate. . . . The chief of this party after having the hatchet stuck in his head, took it out himself and delivered it to the inhuman monster who struck him first, who repeated his stroke a second and a third time, after which the miserable spectacle was dragged by the rope about his neck to the river, thrown in, and suffered to spend still a few moments of life in fruitless strugglings. . . .

Colonel Clarke yet reeking with the blood of those unhappy victims came to the Esplanade [open ground] before the Fort gate, where I had agreed to meet him and treat of the Surrender of the garrison. He spoke with rapture of his late achievement, while he washed off the blood from his hands stain'd in this inhuman sacrifice.

Despite Patriot reprisals against the Iroquois and the Shawnee, Delaware, and other Indian peoples, violence continued along the American frontier until the war's end and beyond. Countless soldiers and settlers died in the Indian wars. But it was the Native Americans who suffered the most, with their ancestral lands scorched and thousands killed by battle, disease, or starvation.

Five

A New Nation

If buttercups buzzed after the bee,

If boats were on land, churches on sea,

If ponies rode men and grass ate the cows,

And cats should be chased to holes by the mouse, . . .

Summer were spring and the t'other way round,

Then all the world would be upside down.

—SONG REPORTEDLY PLAYED DURING THE BRITISH
SURRENDER AT YORKTOWN, OCTOBER 19, 1781

Battle of Monmouth

In the spring of 1778, the Continental army emerged from its hard winter at Valley Forge weary but optimistic. The soldiers were eager to try out the skills learned during the long months of drilling under Baron von Steuben. They soon got their chance.

In June General Henry Clinton, the new commander-in-chief of British forces in America, evacuated Philadelphia. Clinton had decided to relocate his troops to more easily defended New York City. The Continentals marched on Clinton's heels.

They caught up with the Redcoats near Monmouth Court House, New Jersey. In a confusing daylong battle, each side charged, fell back, and rallied again and again. Temperatures soared to 100 degrees, entire squads collapsed from the heat, and nearly one hundred men from both sides died of sunstroke. Finally, the British withdrew. Too exhausted to press their advantage, the Americans let the enemy slip away to safety.

Monmouth was the last major battle of the Revolution fought in the north. For the next three years, Washington's bedraggled army would keep Clinton's forces pinned down in New York with a campaign of small raids and skirmishes. Meanwhile, the main battlefront moved to the south.

THE CONTINENTAL ARMY'S ORDEAL AT VALLEY FORGE IN THE WINTER OF 1777–1778 HAS BECOME A SYMBOL OF COURAGE IN THE FACE OF GREAT SUFFERING. BUT EVEN HARDER WINTERS WOULD FOLLOW, AND THROUGHOUT THE YEAR HUNGER AND NEED WERE THE SOLDIERS' CONSTANT COMPANIONS. FOR MANY SOLDIERS, THE HARDEST PART WAS KNOWING THAT ALL THEIR SUFFERING COULD BE AVOIDED IF ONLY CONGRESS AND THE AMERICAN PEOPLE WOULD DO THEIR PART TO SUPPORT AND SUPPLY THE ARMY. IN A LETTER TO HIS FATHER, CAPTAIN EBENEZER HUNTINGTON OF CONNECTICUT EXPRESSES THE BITTERNESS MANY MEN FELT AS THE HARDSHIPS TOOK THEIR TOLL.

Andrew Huntington Esq.
Norwich
Bush Hutts N Jersey 4 Miles from Pasacik falls
July 7 1780

Dear Sir
. . . The Rascally Stupidity which now prevails in the Country at large, is beyond all descriptions they Patiently see our Illustrious Commander at the Head of 2,500 or 3,000 Ragged tho Virtous & good Men & be oblig'd to put up with what no troops ever did before Why dont you Reinforce your Army, feed them Clothe and pay them, why do you Suffer the Enemy to have a foot hold on the Continent? You Can prevent it, send your Men to the field, believe you are Americans Not suffer yourselves to be dup'd into the thought that the french will relieve you & fight your Battles, it is your own Superiorness

that induc'd Congress to ask foreign Aid, it is a Reflection too much for a Soldier, You dont deserve to be freemen unless you can believe it yourselves, when they arrive they will not put up with such treatment as your Army have done they will not serve Week after Week without Meat without Cloathing, & paid in filthy Rags. I despise My Countrymen. I wish I could say I was not born in America, I once gloried in it but am now ashamed of it—... I have wrote in a Passion, indeed I am scarce ever free from it—I am in Rags, have lain in the Rain on the Ground for 40 hours past, & only a Junk of fresh Beef & that without Salt to dine on this day, rec'd no pay since last December ..., & all this for my Cowardly Countrymen who flinch at the very time when their Exertions are wanted, & hold their Purse Strings as tho they would Damn the World, rather than part with a Dollar to their Army. . . .

Yours
Eb Huntington

Britain's Southern Strategy

Once his troops were settled in New York, General Clinton sent as many men as he could spare to Lord Charles Cornwallis, British commander in the south. Clinton believed that the southern colonies were full of Loyalists who would eagerly support a campaign to crush the rebellion. With their help, Britain could conquer the south and cut off the valuable tobacco shipments that Congress used to pay for war supplies. After that, said one British war leader, "The northern provinces might be left to their own feelings and distress to bring them back to their duty."

Britain's southern campaign began with the capture of Savannah, Georgia. Next a huge force of British, Hessian, and Loyalist troops, supported by one hundred warships, laid siege to Charleston, South Carolina, the south's most important seaport. Charleston held out for six weeks as British artillery pounded the city. "The fire was incessant," wrote one defender, "cannon balls whizzing and shells hissing continually amongst us. . . . It appeared as if the stars were tumbling down."

On May 12, 1780, Charleston surrendered. More than four thousand Americans were taken prisoner and huge stores of weapons and ammunition captured. It was the worst Patriot loss of the war.

British ships guard the waters off Charleston, South Carolina. The entire Patriot army defending the city was forced to surrender after a six-week-long siege.

After the fall of Charleston, the British controlled all of South Carolina and Georgia. A combined French-American expedition to retake Savannah had failed. An attempt to capture Camden, South Carolina, from the British was a "mortifying disaster"—made all the more embarrassing when American General Horatio Gates became one of the first to panic and flee the battlefield. Britain seemed unstoppable. But a new kind of war was just beginning.

Guerrilla Wars

Clinton had been right. The south *was* full of Loyalists. What he hadn't counted on was the equal determination of southern Patriots. As the British moved through the countryside, they were constantly harassed by small bands of rebels. These proud

Benedict Arnold

In 1780, while George Washington struggled to hold together his tattered army up north, Britain was scoring one victory after another in the south. In the midst of these trials came one more piece of bad news: a great American hero had turned traitor.

General Benedict Arnold had been appointed commander of West Point, the Americans' key fortress on the Hudson River. Arnold was a brave, often brilliant military officer who had contributed greatly to the Patriot cause. He was also in secret communication with the British. A proud and resentful man, Arnold believed that Congress had never properly honored or rewarded him for his services. The general was also wildly extravagant and deeply in debt. Greed and bitterness led him to offer the British a deal: he would turn over West Point for a large sum of money.

The plot was uncovered in September 1780 when Major John André, Arnold's British contact, was captured behind American lines. The young British officer was carrying a pass signed by Benedict Arnold, along with detailed plans of West Point's defenses, written in the same handwriting. André was hanged as a spy. Arnold escaped to the British forces in New York City and went on to fight as a general in the British army.

After the war Benedict Arnold lived in England, where the hero-turned-traitor was despised almost as much as he was in America. After all, as one British government official observed, "However you may like the treason it is impossible to approve the traitor."

Benedict Arnold, one of America's finest generals and most famous traitors

Patriot leader Francis Marion invites a captured British officer to share his dinner of sweet potatoes and water. The British called Marion the "Swamp Fox," for his hit-and-run raids, staged from hideouts in South Carolina's watery backcountry.

and independent southerners waged a guerrilla war—approaching suddenly, striking fast, then melting back into the forests and swamps. One band of guerrillas surprised Loyalists who were rounding up cattle for the British army, taking seventy prisoners. Another group of seventeen mounted rebels staged a lightning raid on British and Loyalist troops marching American prisoners of war to Charleston. The Patriots, led by Francis Marion, known as the "Swamp Fox," freed the prisoners and transferred their chains to the new captives.

In October 1780 Cornwallis's army advanced into North Carolina. One branch of the army, made up of 1,100 Loyalists, marched along the western frontier. On a wooded hill called Kings Mountain, one mile south of the North Carolina border, they met a force of buckskin-clad riflemen. Sixteen-year-old Patriot James Collins was "in profuse sweat" as he joined the rebel attack on the Loyalist forces.

We soon attempted to climb the hill, but were fiercely charged upon and forced to fall back to our first position. We tried a second time, but met the same fate; the fight then seemed to become more furious. . . . We took to the hill a third time; the enemy gave way. When we had gotten near the top, some of our leaders roared out, "Hurrah, my brave fellows! Advance! They are crying for quarter!"

The rebel victory at Kings Mountain halted the British advance through the south. Cornwallis was forced to withdraw his remaining troops into South Carolina and wait for reinforcements. British General Clinton would later call the battle "the first link of a chain of evils that followed each other in regular succession until they at last ended in the total loss of America."

Backcountry Adventures

On the day of the Patriot victory at Kings Mountain, Washington appointed Nathanael Greene to replace General Gates as commander of southern forces. It was no cushy assignment. The Continentals were sickly and half-starved, dressed in rags, many without shoes. "The wants of this army are so numerous and various," the new commander told a friend back north, "that the shortest way of telling you is to inform you that we have nothing."

Wisely, General Greene decided to avoid an all-out confrontation with the British. Instead, he would use his army to support the guerrilla tactics of southern Patriots. One by one, mingled Continental, militia, and guerrilla forces picked off British supply wagons and outposts. After each encounter the Redcoats chased the rebels through the swamps and woods, only to give up after a few days of mud and mosquitoes.

In January 1781 British and Loyalist forces led by the ruthless cavalry officer Banastre Tarleton caught up with Daniel Morgan and the Patriots at a field called the Cowpens, in South Carolina. The rebels turned and made a stand, giving Tarleton's troops "a devil of a whipping." Two months later, the Americans and British met again, at Guilford Court House, North Carolina. In several hours of savage fighting, the rebels killed nearly one-quarter of Cornwallis's army.

By now Cornwallis was "quite tired of marching about the country in quest of adventures." His tired, battered troops had little to show for more than a year of hard backcountry campaigning. Southern Loyalist support had evaporated, and every tree and brier patch seemed to hide a rebel. In early spring the British general decided to take his troops to Virginia.

Victory at Yorktown

As Cornwallis marched north, the mood in Washington's camp outside New York City was gloomy. The Continental army had suffered through another winter without decent food, clothes, or housing. The bright hopes raised by the alliance with France had turned sour. French troops had arrived in America but so far they had seen little fighting, and the early actions of the French fleet were dismal failures. In Virginia Benedict Arnold was leading British forces on a campaign of terror and destruction, while Lafayette, sent with a small army to stop him, reported that his men were "not strong enough even to get beaten."

ON THE EVE OF THE BATTLE OF YORKTOWN, THE PATRIOT CAUSE LOOKED ALMOST HOPELESS. IN THIS LETTER TO HIS SON GEORGE, LIVING IN FRANCE, GEORGE MASON OF VIRGINIA OUTLINES THE OBSTACLES: BRITAIN'S CONTROL OF THE COASTAL WATERWAYS, CONTINUING SHORTAGES IN THE CONTINENTAL ARMY, LOSSES INFLICTED BY BENEDICT ARNOLD AND CORNWALLIS, AND THE DISAPPOINTING PERFORMANCE OF AMERICA'S FRENCH ALLIES.

[1781]

. . . Our affairs have been, for some time, growing from bad to worse. The enemy's fleet commands our rivers, and puts it in their power to remove their troops, from place to place, when and where they please without opposition; so that we no sooner collect a force sufficient to counteract them in one part of the country, but they shift to another, ravaging, plundering, and destroying every thing before them. Our militia turn out with great spirit, and have, in several late actions, behaved bravely, but they are badly armed and appointed [supplied]. General Green with about 1200 regular troops and some militia, is in South Carolina; where he has taken all the enemy's posts, except Charleston.

. . . Lord Cornwallis, quitting North Carolina, has since joined Arnold, with about 1200 infantry and 300 cavalry, and taken the chief command of their army in Virginia, now consisting of about 5000 men. They . . . burnt Page's warehouses, where the greatest part of the York River tobacco was collected; they had before burned most of the tobacco upon James river, and have plundered great part of the adjacent country. . . .

We have had various accounts of the sailing of a French fleet, with a body of land forces, for America; should they really arrive it would quickly change the face of our affairs. . . .

God bless you, my dear child; and grant that we may again meet, in your native country, as freemen;—otherwise, that we may never see each other more, is the prayer of

Your affectionate father,
G. Mason

Then came the opportunity Washington had been praying for. A new French fleet, just arrived from the West Indies, was sailing for Chesapeake Bay. Cornwallis's army was in Yorktown, Virginia, a small port near the mouth of the Chesapeake. If the Americans and French acted quickly, they just might catch the British in a trap.

On August 21, 1781, the allied armies left New York. Sixteen days later, after a march of 250 miles, the first troops stumbled into Virginia. The French fleet had driven off the British navy, leaving Cornwallis with no hope of escaping or receiving reinforcements by sea. The allies immediately set to work cutting off his escape by land.

"We now began to make preparations for laying close siege to the enemy," wrote Joseph Plumb Martin. "We had holed him and nothing remained but to dig him out." The allies dug long trenches and dragged in their heavy artillery. On October 9, Martin was among the thousands gathered in the trenches.

> All were upon the tiptoe of expectation and impatience to see the signal given to open the whole line of batteries, which was to be the hoisting of the American flag in the ten-gun battery. About noon the much-wished-for signal went up. I confess I felt a secret pride swell my heart when I saw the "star-spangled banner" waving majestically in the very faces of our implacable adversaries. . . . A simultaneous discharge of all the guns in the line followed, the French troops accompanying it with "Huzza for the Americans!"

George Washington surveys the besieged city of Yorktown, Virginia. British troops inside the city were surrounded by American and French forces on land and in the sea.

For days the attackers' big guns pounded the enemy's defenses. The nonstop bombardment was so loud and furious that, to one Hessian officer, it seemed "as though the heavens should split." The British fell back under the devastating fire, and the allies pushed closer. Inside Yorktown houses were smashed to rubble and hundreds of soldiers were killed or badly wounded. On October 17 a redcoated drummer boy climbed a wall, beating the signal for a truce. "I thought I never heard a drum equal to it," said Continental lieutenant Ebenezer Denny, "the most delightful music to us all."

Two days later, the allies formed two facing lines outside the smoking ruins of Yorktown. On one side were the French, in their handsome uniforms. On the other stood the Americans who, observed Continental surgeon James Thacher, "though not all in uniform, nor their dress so neat, yet exhibited an erect, soldierly air." As a

The British army surrenders at Yorktown, October 19, 1781.

British military band played, some seven thousand Redcoats filed past and threw down their weapons. One of the tunes reportedly played was the old English ballad "The World Turned Upside Down."

"Many Dangers Past"

Yorktown was the last major battle of the American Revolution. Although Britain still had 30,000 troops in America, the British people were demanding an end to

American-born artist Benjamin West started this painting of the signing of the Treaty of Paris with portraits of the American delegation; (from right to left): William Temple Franklin, Henry Laurens, Benjamin Franklin, John Adams, and John Jay. When the British delegates refused to pose, West's painting was left forever unfinished.

the fight. In early 1782 Parliament voted for peace, and Benjamin Franklin, John Jay, and John Adams went to Paris to negotiate an agreement. On September 3, 1783, Great Britain and the United States signed the Treaty of Paris, formally ending the war. The treaty recognized U.S. independence and extended the boundaries of the new nation west to the Mississippi River.

27 July 1783

Dear Sir,

. . . I join with you most cordially in rejoicing at the return of Peace. I hope it will be lasting, and that Mankind will at length, as they call themselves reasonable Creatures, have Reason and Sense enough to settle their Differences without cutting Throats; for in my opinion there never was a good War, or a bad Peace.

What vast additions to the Conveniences and Comforts of Living might Mankind have acquired, if the Money spent in Wars had been employ'd in Works of public utility! What an extension of Agriculture, even to the Tops of our Mountains; what Rivers rendered navigable, or joined by Canals; what Bridges, Aqueducts, new Roads, and other public Works, Edifices, and Improvements, rendering England a compleat Paradise, might have been obtain'd by spending those Millions in doing good, which in the last War have been spent in doing Mischief; in bringing Misery into thousands of Families, and destroying the Lives of so many thousands of working people who might have perform'd the useful labour! . . .

I [am] your most obedient and most humble servant,
B. Franklin

Washington embraces General Henry Knox, commander of the Continental artillery, at his farewell dinner with his officers, December 1783.

In December 1783 George Washington said an emotional farewell to his remaining officers in New York City. Similar scenes of parting had been taking place for months throughout America. After Yorktown many soldiers had deserted or gone home as their enlistments expired. A few months before the peace treaty was finalized, Washington began sending the remaining enlisted men home. Joseph Plumb Martin's regiment was disbanded in June.

> I confess, after all, that my anticipation of the happiness I should experience upon such a day as this was not realized; . . . there was as much sorrow as joy transfused on the occasion. We had lived together as a family of brothers for several years, . . . like

most other families, had shared with each other the hardships, dangers, and sufferings incident to a soldier's life. . . . And now we were to be, the greater part of us, parted forever.

Martin settled in the part of Massachusetts that would later become Maine and lived out his life as a respected farmer and laborer. At age seventy he wrote an account of his adventures as a Continental soldier, ending with these verses:

Through much fatigue and many dangers past,
The warworn soldier's braved his way at last.

Conclusion

The Fruits of Liberty

The American Revolution was over. The hard work of building a nation had just begun. The Articles of Confederation, ratified in 1781, had created a weak and ineffective national government. In 1787 delegates to a constitutional convention threw out the articles and drafted a new document. The Constitution of the United States, which went into effect two years later, created a strong central government, with its power derived from the people. In 1791 Congress passed the Bill of Rights, the first ten amendments to the Constitution, guaranteeing certain fundamental freedoms. With the addition of the Bill of Rights, the Constitution fulfilled the spirit of the Revolution: creating a "more perfect union" and protecting individual liberties.

Not everyone shared in the fruits of liberty. The persecution of Loyalists continued for many years after the war. Somewhere between 60,000 and 100,000 Loyalists fled America during and just after the Revolution, and many who tried to return met with hatred and violence. American women, who had contributed much to the war effort, remained second-class citizens after the Revolution, with few legal rights and few paths open to them beyond the roles of wife and mother. Native Americans—no matter which side they had supported—faced continuing bloodshed and loss as white settlers pushed the frontier west.

African Americans, too, found that the Revolutionary ideals of liberty and equality did not apply to them. Thousands of slaves who had fought for the Patriots or the British did win their freedom. Several northern states did pass laws calling for the immediate or gradual abolition of slavery. But in the South the institution of slavery became stronger than ever. It would take eighty years and another terrible war for America to answer the challenge posed by a group of New Hampshire slaves in 1776: to ensure "that the name of slave may not more be heard in a land gloriously contending for the sweets of freedom."

One historian has called the American Revolution "a time of planting rather than harvest." When the smoke of battle cleared, many contradictions and conflicts confronted the new nation. But the seeds of sweeping change had been planted. The Revolutionaries had waged a war for independence and established the first representative democracy. New generations of Americans would come to see liberty and equality as their birthright and fight to make these ideals a reality. Inspired by America's enduring example, the peoples of other nations would also rise up against tyranny. "The eyes of the whole world are turned upon [the United States]," said George Washington at the war's end. "With our fate will the destiny of unborn Millions be involved."

Time Line of Revolutionary War Events

1765

MARCH 22

Parliament passes the Stamp Act, the first direct tax on the American colonies.

1766

MARCH 18

Parliament repeals the Stamp Act.

1767

JUNE 29

Parliament passes the Townshend Acts, imposing duties on many goods imported into the colonies.

1768

OCTOBER 1

Two British regiments arrive in Boston.

1770	1773	1774	1775
MARCH 5 The "Boston Massacre": Five civilians are killed in a confrontation with British soldiers in Boston.	MAY 10 Parliament passes the Tea Act, allowing the British East India Company to bypass export duties (but not taxes) and sell its tea cheaply in the colonies.	MARCH 31– JUNE 22 Parliament passes the Coercive Acts (called the Intolerable Acts in America) to punish Massachusetts for the Boston Tea Party.	APRIL 19 Battles of Lexington and Concord.
	DECEMBER 16 The Boston Tea Party: Colonists disguised as Indians board three merchant ships in Boston Harbor and dump 342 chests of tea into the water.	SEPTEMBER 5– OCTOBER 26 The First Continental Congress meets in Philadelphia.	MAY 10 The Second Continental Congress opens in Philadelphia. Colonial forces capture Fort Ticonderoga.
			JUNE 15 Congress names George Washington commander-in-chief of the newly formed Continental army.
			JUNE 17 Battle of Bunker Hill in Boston.
			OCTOBER 13 Congress creates the Continental navy.
			NOVEMBER 13 American forces under Montgomery capture Montreal.
			DECEMBER 31 Battle of Quebec.

1776

JANUARY 9
Thomas Paine's *Common Sense* is published.

MARCH 17
The British evacuate Boston after an American siege that began April 19, 1775.

JULY 4
Congress adopts the Declaration of Independence.

AUGUST 27
Battle of Long Island, New York.

SEPTEMBER 15
The British occupy New York City.

DECEMBER 25–26
Washington crosses the Delaware River into New Jersey and captures Trenton.

1777

JANUARY 3
Washington and the Continental army win the Battle of Princeton, New Jersey.

SEPTEMBER 11
Battle of Brandywine Creek, Pennsylvania.

SEPTEMBER 23
The British occupy Philadelphia, as Congress flees the city.

OCTOBER 17
British General John Burgoyne surrenders to American General Horatio Gates at Saratoga, New York.

1778

FEBRUARY 6
France signs a treaty of alliance with the United States, entering the war against Britain.

JUNE 16–18
The British evacuate Philadelphia and begin a march toward New York City.

JUNE 28
Battle of Monmouth, New Jersey.

DECEMBER 29
The British capture Savannah, Georgia.

1779

SEPTEMBER 23
John Paul Jones, commanding the *Bonhomme Richard*, captures the British warship *Serapis* off the coast of England.

OCTOBER 9
A French and American attempt to recapture Savannah fails.

1780	1781	1782	1783
MAY 12 The British capture Charleston, South Carolina. AUGUST 16 British forces under General Charles Cornwallis defeat American forces under Gates at Camden, South Carolina. SEPTEMBER 25 Benedict Arnold's plot to surrender West Point to the British is discovered. OCTOBER 7 American frontiersmen defeat a British-led Loyalist army at Kings Mountain, South Carolina, halting Cornwallis's advance through the south.	JANUARY 17 Battle of the Cowpens, South Carolina: Daniel Morgan leads Continentals and militiamen to victory over a British and Loyalist army under Banastre Tarleton. MARCH 1 Congress adopts the Articles of Confederation, establishing the first U.S. government. MARCH 15 The British win a costly victory at Guilford Court House, South Carolina, losing one-quarter of Cornwallis's army. OCTOBER 19 Cornwallis surrenders to Washington at Yorktown, Virginia: the last major battle of the Revolutionary War.	JULY 11 British troops evacuate Savannah. OCTOBER 1 Peace negotiations begin in Paris, with Benjamin Franklin, John Adams, and John Jay representing the United States. DECEMBER 14 The British evacuate Charleston.	SEPTEMBER 3 The Treaty of Paris is signed, formally ending the Revolutionary War.

Glossary

boycott To protest by refusing to buy goods from a business or a nation.

cavalry An army mounted on horseback.

garrison A military post, or the troops stationed there.

grenadiers Members of a regiment of British or Hessian soldiers specially chosen for their superior strength and ability.

guerrilla A fighter in a kind of warfare that uses small groups that can move and strike quickly, then disappear into the surrounding countryside.

Hessians German soldiers-for-hire who fought for the British in the Revolutionary War; most came from the German state of Hesse.

Iroquois League A confederation of six Native American peoples of New York, the Mohawk, Oneida, Onondaga, Cayuga, Seneca, and Tuscarora, also called the Six Nations; all but the Oneida and Tuscarora sided with the British in the Revolutionary War.

light infantry Troops that were lightly equipped so they could move and attack quickly.

mercenaries Soldiers hired to fight for the army of another country.

Parliament The legislative body of Great Britain.

privateer A privately owned ship licensed by the government in times of war to attack enemy shipping.

siege A military blockade of a fort or city, intended to cut off food and other supplies and force a surrender.

treason The crime of trying to overthrow the government of one's own country.

To Find Out More

BOOKS

Beller, Susan Provost. *American Voices from the Revolutionary War.* New York: Benchmark Books, 2003.
Part of a series that explores American history through the use of primary sources.

———. *The Revolutionary War.* New York: Benchmark Books, 2002.
This book's companion volume in the Letters from the Homefront series.

Gay, Kathlyn, and Martin Gay. *Revolutionary War.* Voices from the Past series. New York: Henry Holt, 1995.
Covers the major battles of the Revolution, weaving in personal accounts by soldiers and civilians.

Littlefield, Daniel C. *Revolutionary Citizens: African Americans, 1776–1804.* Vol. 3 of *The Young Oxford History of African Americans.* New York: Oxford University Press, 1997.
Looks at the war from the point of view of African Americans, including slaves, free men and women, and soldiers who fought on both sides of the conflict.

Marrin, Albert. *The War for Independence: The Story of the American Revolution*. New York: Atheneum, 1988.
Interestingly written, with lots of useful information and stories about the people who commanded and fought in the Revolution.

Meltzer, Milton. *The American Revolutionaries: A History in Their Own Words, 1750–1800*. New York: Thomas Y. Crowell, 1987.
Recaptures the "human experience" of the Revolution through letters, diaries, memoirs, and other first-person narratives of life in late-eighteenth-century America.

Nardo, Don. *The American Revolution*. Opposing Viewpoints Digests series. San Diego, CA: Greenhaven Press, 1998.
Explores war issues from the point of view of both Patriots and Loyalists and includes several long excerpts from Revolutionary-era documents.

Weber, Michael. *The American Revolution*. The Making of America series. Austin, TX: Raintree Steck-Vaughn, 2000.
A clear, thorough account of war events, with many good photographs.

ON THE INTERNET*

"The American Revolution." © 2001–2003, at http://theamericanrevolution.org/index.htm
This website offers articles on important people, places, and events in the American Revolution, plus historical documents and a time line. Click on "Battles" for information on major engagements, including dates, casualties, commanders, strategies, and even the weather conditions.

"The American Revolution: The Struggle for Independence" at http://patriot.history/1700s.com
Articles on this site cover a variety of topics related to the Revolution, plus a time line, links to other sources, and homework tips.

"The History Place: American Revolution" at http://www.historyplace.com/unitedstates/revolution/index.html
A detailed and easy-to-use time line of events leading up to and through the Revolution.

"Liberty! The American Revolution" © 1997 PBS Online and Twin Cities Public
    Television, at http://www.pbs.org/ktca/liberty
This on-line companion to the six-part PBS series Liberty! *includes lots of information plus an interactive game that takes you on a interesting (and often funny) step-by-step journey through the Revolution.*

"The Revolutionary War: A Journey towards Freedom" at http://library.thinkquest.org/
    10966/index.html
Created by students for the 1997 ThinkQuest Internet Challenge, this site offers illustrated tours of Valley Forge and Washington's crossing of the Delaware, plus biographies and important documents. Click on "Fun Zone" for links to games, including a strategy/war game that lets you command British or American forces in battle against other players on your computer or via the internet.

*Websites change from time to time. For additional on-line information, check with the media specialist at your local library.

Bibliography

Axelrod, Alan. *The Complete Idiot's Guide to the American Revolution.* Indianapolis, IN: Alpha Books, 2000.

Beebe, Lewis. *Journal of Dr. Lewis Beebe.* New York: New York Times and Arno Press, 1971.

Butterfield, L. H., Marc Friedlaender, and Mary-Jo Kline. *The Book of Abigail and John: Selected Letters of the Adams Family, 1762–1784.* Cambridge, MA: Harvard University Press, 1975.

Commager, Henry Steele, and Richard B. Morris, eds. *The Spirit of 'Seventy-Six: The Story of the American Revolution as Told by Participants.* New York: Da Capo Press, 1995.

Crary, Catherine S. *The Price of Loyalty: Tory Writings from the Revolutionary Era.* New York: McGraw-Hill, 1973.

Dudley, William, ed. *The American Revolution: Opposing Viewpoints.* San Diego, CA: Greenhaven Press, 1992.

Editors of Time-Life Books. *The Revolutionaries.* Alexandria, VA: Time-Life Books, 1996.

Fleming, Thomas. *Liberty! The American Revolution.* New York: Viking, 1997.

"George Washington Papers at the Library of Congress, 1741–1799" at http://lcweb2.lcweb2.loc.gov/ammem/gwhtml/gwhome.html

Hulton, Ann. *Letters of a Loyalist Lady.* New York: New York Times and Arno Press, 1971.

Jones, Thomas. *History of New York during the Revolutionary War.* New York: New-York Historical Society, 1879.

Lancaster, Bruce. *The American Heritage Book of the Revolution.* New York: American Heritage, 1971.

Martin, Joseph Plumb. *Private Yankee Doodle: Being a Narrative of Some of the Adventures, Dangers and Sufferings of a Revolutionary Soldier.* Edited by George F. Scheer. Boston: Little, Brown, 1962.

Morison, Samuel Eliot, ed. *Sources and Documents Illustrating the American Revolution, 1764–1788.* New York: Oxford University Press, 1972.

Niles, H[ezekiah]. *Principles and Acts of the Revolution in America.* Baltimore: William Ogden Niles, 1822.

Paine, Thomas. *Common Sense.* Patchogue, NY: Buccaneer Books, 1976.

Purcell, L. Edward, and David F. Burg. *The World Almanac of the American Revolution.* New York: World Almanac, 1992.

Randel, William Peirce. *The American Revolution: Mirror of a People.* Maplewood, NJ: Hammond, 1973.

Scott, John Anthony. *Trumpet of a Prophecy: Revolutionary America, 1763–1783.* New York: Knopf, 1969.

Sobol, Donald J., ed. *An American Revolutionary War Reader.* New York: Franklin Watts, 1964.

Tallmadge, Benjamin. *Memoir of Colonel Benjamin Tallmadge.* New York: New York Times and Arno Press, 1968.

Thacher, James. *Military Journal of the American Revolution.* New York: New York Times and Arno Press, 1969.

Werner, Kirk D., ed. *The American Revolution.* San Diego, CA: Greenhaven, 2000.

Wheeler, Richard. *Voices of 1776.* New York: Thomas Y. Crowell, 1972.

Winslow, Eugene. *Afro-Americans '76: Black Americans in the Founding of Our Nation.* Chicago: Afro-Am Publishing, 1975.

The World Almanac and Book of Facts 2002. Mahwah, NJ: World Almanac Books, 2002.

Young, Alfred F., Terry J. Fife, and Mary E. Janzen. *We the People: Voices and Images of the New Nation.* Philadelphia: Temple University Press, 1993.

Notes on Quotes

The quotations in this book are from the following sources:

Introduction: The Seeds of Revolution
p. 7, "War is inevitable": Commager and Morris, *Spirit of 'Seventy-Six,* pp. 108, 109.

Chapter One: The Shot Heard 'Round the World
p. 8, "When I reflect": ibid., p. 76.
p. 12, "ready to act": Weber, *American Revolution,* p. 25.
p. 12, "The militia could not": Fleming, *Liberty!,* p. 197.
p. 13, "We were fired at": ibid., p. 87.
p. 13, "cruel aggression": Morison, *Sources and Documents,* p. 143.
p. 15, "preposterous parade": Wheeler, *Voices of 1776,* p. 35.
p. 16, "the rebels hove down": Jones, *History of New York,* p. 52.
p. 16, "If we have eight": Sobol, *American Revolutionary War Reader,* p. 24.
p. 18, "Good God": Fleming, *Liberty!,* p. 165.
p. 18, "a restoration": Commager and Morris, *Spirit of 'Seventy-Six,* p. 271.
p. 19, "Our own happiness": Editors of Time-Life, *Revolutionaries,* p. 75.
p. 19, "Britain is the parent": Paine, *Common Sense,* pp. 41, 46, 73.
p. 19, "but *Common Sense*" and "the dictates": Young and Fife, *We the People,* p. 51.
p. 19, "happy talent": Commager and Morris, *Spirit of 'Seventy-Six,* p. 313.
p. 21, "perpetual itching": Marrin, *War for Independence,* p. 88.
p. 21, "a triple," "drums beating," and "very solemn": Scott, *Trumpet of a Prophecy,* p. 127.
p. 21, "There must be" and "Yes, we must": Fleming, *Liberty!,* p. 176.

Chapter Two: Loyalists versus Patriots
p. 22, "Neighbor was against Neighbor": Weber, *American Revolution,* p. 47.
p. 22, "middle third": Commager and Morris, *Spirit of 'Seventy-Six,* p. 325.
p. 23, "Freemen contending": Nardo, *American Revolution,* p. 90.

p. 24, "Nothing . . . ever hurt me": Editors of Time-Life, *Revolutionaries*, p. 100.

p. 27, "Anarchy, & Violence": Crary, *Price of Loyalty*, p. 19.

p. 27, "proceeded not": ibid., p. 104.

p. 27, "a thing whose head": Marrin, *War for Independence*, p. 90.

p. 27, "infamous betrayers": Commager and Morris, *Spirit of 'Seventy-Six,* p. 333.

p. 28, "cool his loyalty": Crary, *Price of Loyalty,* p. 57.

p. 28, "every low-lived wretch": Wheeler, *Voices of 1776,* p. 92.

p. 29, "The committee proposed": Crary, *Price of Loyalty,* pp. 82–83.

p. 29, "We had some Grand": Jones, *History of New York,* pp. 596–597.

p. 29, "carried upon a Rail": Crary, *Price of Loyalty,* pp. 57–58.

p. 29, "I believe that committees": ibid., p. 148.

p. 32, "The worst which can": Commager and Morris, *Spirit of 'Seventy-Six,* p. 346.

Chapter Three: Yankee Doodle on Land and Sea

p. 33, "The horses attached": Commager and Morris, *Spirit of 'Seventy-Six,* p. 519.

p. 33 "an exceeding dirty": Fleming, *Liberty!,* p. 148.

p. 36, "These are the times": Commager and Morris, *Spirit of 'Seventy-Six,* p. 505.

p. 36, "It was as severe": Editors of Time-Life, *Revolutionaries,* p. 92.

p. 39, "The enemy have fled": Niles, *Chronicles,* p. 342.

p. 39, "the general opinion": Martin, *Private Yankee Doodle,* p. 59.

p. 41, "they left their kettles": ibid., p. 73.

p. 41, "Morgan . . . poured down": Commager and Morris, *Spirit of 'Seventy-Six,* p. 592.

p. 41, "with a voice": Editors of Time-Life, *Revolutionaries,* p. 111.

p. 42, "good and faithful": Scott, *Trumpet of a Prophecy,* p. 228.

p. 42, "We arrived" and "the greatest part": Martin, *Private Yankee Doodle,* pp. 101–102.

p. 45, "Yankee Doodle came to town": Marrin, *War for Independence,* p. 26.

p. 45, "Yankee Doodle is the tune": Fleming, *Liberty!,* p. 125.

p. 46, "the patient fortitude": Fleming, *Liberty!,* p. 280.

p. 46, "I have not yet": Commager and Morris, *Spirit of 'Seventy-Six,* p. 948.

p. 47, "serve their Country": Marrin, *War for Independence,* p. 177.

p. 50, "shrunken and decayed": Commager and Morris, *Spirit of 'Seventy-Six,* p. 858.

p. 50, "covered with dirt": Scott, *Trumpet of a Prophecy,* p. 171.

p. 50, "silence was a stranger": ibid., p. 173.

Chapter Four: Americans All

p. 51, "If there be an object": Randel, *American Revolution,* pp. 30–31.

p. 53, "No regiment": Winslow, *Afro-Americans,* p. 39.

p. 55, "essential service": ibid., p. 54.

p. 57, "Proceed, great chief": Littlefield, *Revolutionary Citizens,* p. 35.

p. 57, "heard the roar": Werner, *American Revolution,* p. 198.

p. 58, "as scouts": Commager and Morris, *Spirit of 'Seventy-Six,* p. 1003.

p. 58, "loose the savages": Marrin, *War for Independence,* p. 184.

p. 58, "The flames": Commager and Morris, *Spirit of 'Seventy-Six,* p. 1010.

p. 58, "they proceeded": Wheeler, *Voices of 1776,* p. 283.

p. 59, "a single settlement": Axelrod, *Complete Idiot's Guide,* p. 262.

p. 59, "When your army": Editors of Time-Life, *Revolutionaries,* p. 129.

Chapter Five: A New Nation

p. 61, "If buttercups buzzed": Commager and Morris, *Spirit of 'Seventy-Six,* p. 1246.

p. 63, "The northern provinces": ibid., p. 1075.

p. 63, "The fire was incessant," Wheeler, *Voices of 1776,* p. 329.

p. 64, "mortifying disaster": ibid., p. 338.

p. 65, "However you may like": Commager and Morris, *Spirit of 'Seventy-Six,* p. 746.

p. 66, "in profuse sweat": ibid., p. 1144.

p. 67, "the first link": Purcell and Burg, *World Almanac,* p. 253.

p. 67, "The wants": Commager and Morris, *Spirit of 'Seventy-Six,* p. 1152.

p. 67, "a devil": Editors of Time-Life, *Revolutionaries,* p. 145.

p. 68, "quite tired": Commager and Morris, *Spirit of 'Seventy-Six,* p. 1201.

p. 68, "not strong enough": ibid., p. 1204.

p. 69, "We now began": Martin, *Private Yankee Doodle,* p. 230.

p. 69, "All were upon": ibid., p. 233.

p. 71, "as though the heavens": Editors of Time-Life, *Revolutionaries,* p. 164.

p. 71, "I thought I never": ibid., p. 165.

p. 71, "though not all": Thacher, *Military Journal,* p. 289.

p. 74, "I confess": Martin, *Private Yankee Doodle,* p. 280.

p. 75, "Through much fatigue": ibid., p. 294.

Conclusion: The Fruits of Liberty

p. 77, "that the name": Weber, *American Revolution,* p. 67.

p. 77, "a time of planting": Dudley, *American Revolution,* p. 241.

p. 77, "The eyes": Commager and Morris, *Spirit of 'Seventy-Six,* p. 1287.

Acknowledgments

Every effort has been made to trace the copyright holders of letters and other personal writings reprinted in this book. We apologize for any omissions or errors in this regard and would be pleased to make the appropriate acknowledgments in any future printings.

Grateful acknowledgments are made to the following historical societies, libraries, and publishers:

Francis Smith to Thomas Gage, April 22, 1775; John Adams to Abigail Adams, July 3, 1776; and Abigail Adams to John Adams, July 31, 1777. Reprinted by permission of the Massachusetts Historical Society.

Jonas Clark sermon, April 19, 1776. From the collection of the Lexington, Massachusetts, Historical Society.

George Washington to Martha Washington, June 18, 1775. From Chase, Philander D., ed. *The Papers of George Washington.* Charlottesville, VA: University Press of Virginia, 1985. Courtesy of the Alderman Library, University of Virginia.

Benedict Arnold to Philip Schuyler, November 27, 1775. Collections of Maine Historical Society.

Speech by a farmer of Philadelphia, May 1776; and George Mason to his son George, 1781. From Niles, Hezekiah. *Principles and Acts of the Revolution in America.* Baltimore: William Ogden Niles, 1822.

Jacob Duché to George Washington, October 8, 1777. George Washington Papers, Manuscript Division, Series 4, Library of Congress.

Ann Hulton to Mrs. Lightbody, January 31, 1774. Courtesy of the Harvard University Press.

William Emerson to his wife, July 17, 1775. From French, Allen. *The First Year of the American Revolution.* New York: Octagon Books, 1968.

Henry Knox to his wife, December 28, 1776. From Drake, Francis S., ed. *Life and Correspondence of Henry Knox.* Boston: Samuel G. Drake, 1873.

Henry Clinton to John Burgoyne, August 1777. William L. Clements Library, University of Michigan.

John Greenwood narrative, 1779. From Greenwood, John. *A Young Patriot in the American Revolution, 1775–1783: The Wartime Services of John Greenwood.* New York: Westvaco Corp., 1981.

Peter Bestes, Sambo Freeman, Felix Holbrook, and Chester Joie to the Massachusetts Legislature, April 20, 1773. Collection of the New-York Historical Society.

Henry Hamilton narrative, February 23, 1779. From *Report of the Pioneer Society of the State of Michigan,* vol. 9, 2nd ed. Lansing, MI: Wynkoop, Hallenbeck, Crawford Co., 1908.

Ebenezer Huntington to Andrew Huntington, July 7, 1780. From Huntington, Ebenezer. *Letters Written by Ebenezer Huntington during the American Revolution.* New York: Chas. Fred. Heartman, 1915. Courtesy of the Connecticut Historical Society.

Benjamin Franklin to Joseph Banks, July 27, 1783. By permission of the British Library.

Index

Page numbers for illustrations are in boldface

About the Author

"After researching and writing books for the *Letters from the Homefront* series, it was fascinating to take a look at America's wars from a different point of view in *Letters from the Battlefront.* While I read the letters, diaries, and reflections of soldiers from the American Revolution all the way through the Vietnam War, I was struck once again by the way, in our fast-changing world, people themselves remain so little changed. The Continental soldier shivering at Valley Forge and the army infantryman in the jungles of South Vietnam wore different uniforms and carried different weapons. They sometimes used different words to express their feelings. But beneath the skin, their basic concerns and emotions—their love of life, their longing for home and family, their search for meaning amid the bewildering inhumanity of war—were startlingly similar."

VIRGINIA SCHOMP has written more than forty books on nonfiction topics including ancient cultures and American history. Ms. Schomp lives in the Catskill Mountain region of New York with her husband, Richard, and their son, Chip.